PRECARIOUS LIFE

PRECARIOUS LIFE

THE POWERS OF MOURNING AND VIOLENCE

JUDITH BUTLER

VERSO

London • New York

This paperback edition first published by Verso 2020
First published by Verso 2004
© Judith Butler 2004, 2006, 2020

The moral rights of the author have been asserted

1 3 5 7 9 10 8 6 4 2

Verso
UK: 6 Meard Street, London W1F 0EG
US: 20 Jay Street, Suite 1010, Brooklyn, NY 11201
versobooks.com

Verso is the imprint of New Left Books

ISBN-13: 978-1-78873-861-3

British Library Cataloguing in Publication Data
A catalogue record for this book is available from the British Library

Library of Congress Has Cataloged the Hardcover as follows:
Butler, Judith.
    Precarious life: the powers of mourning and violence / Judith Butler.
        p. cm.
    Includes bibliographical references and index.
    ISBN 1–84467–005–8 (hardback: alk. paper)
    1. War on Terrorism, 2001 – Moral and ethical aspects. 2. Violence – Political
aspects – United States. 3. Nationalism – United States. 4. Mass media and public
opinion – United States. 5. United States – Foreign relations – 21st century.
I. Title.

HV6432.B88 2003
303.6—dc22

Typeset in Fournier
Printed and bound by CPI Group (UK) Ltd, Croydon CR0 4YY

For Isaac,
who imagines otherwise

CONTENTS

ACKNOWLEDGMENTS

I am grateful to the Guggenheim Foundation and the Princeton University Center for Human Values for funding the 2001–02 academic year when work on these essays began. I also thank Amy Jamgochian for her patient and thorough work on the manuscript and Benjamin Young and Stuart Murray for their helpful work. Wendy Brown and Joan Scott read many of these words, and their extraordinary persistence as vigorous interlocutors has been crucial to the completing of this work.

"Explanation and Exoneration" appeared first in *Theory and Event*, 5:4, and was reprinted in *Social Text*, no. 72. "Violence, Mourning, Politics" appeared first in *Studies in Gender and Sexuality*, 4:1, and represents a reworked version of the Kessler Lecture delivered in December, 2001 at the Center of Lesbian and Gay Studies at CUNY. "Indefinite Detention" appeared first in a reduced form in Victor

Goldberg, ed., *It's a Free Country: Personal Liberties after 9/11*, New York: RMD Press, 2002; an earlier version appeared in part as "Guantanamo Limbo," in the *Nation*, April 1, 2002. "The Charge of Anti-Semitism" was published in reduced form by the *London Review of Books*, August 21, 2003.

PREFACE

The five essays collected here were all written after September 11, 2001, and in response to the conditions of heightened vulnerability and aggression that followed from those events. It was my sense in the fall of 2001 that the United States was missing an opportunity to redefine itself as part of a global community when, instead, it heightened nationalist discourse, extended surveillance mechanisms, suspended constitutional rights, and developed forms of explicit and implicit censorship. These events led public intellectuals to waver in their public commitment to principles of justice and prompted journalists to take leave of the time-honored tradition of investigative journalism. That US boundaries were breached, that an unbearable vulnerability was exposed, that a terrible toll on human life was taken, were, and are, cause for fear and for mourning; they are also instigations for patient political reflection. These events posed the question, implicitly at least, as to what form political reflection and deliberation ought to take if we take injurability and aggression as two points of departure for political life.

That we can be injured, that others can be injured, that we are subject to death at the whim of another, are all reasons for both fear and grief. What is less certain, however, is whether the experiences of vulnerability and loss have to lead straightaway to military violence and retribution. There are other passages. If we are interested in arresting cycles of violence to produce less violent outcomes, it is no doubt important to ask what, politically, might be made of grief besides a cry for war.

One insight that injury affords is that there are others out there on whom my life depends, people I do not know and may never know. This fundamental dependency on anonymous others is not a condition that I can will away. No security measure will foreclose this dependency; no violent act of sovereignty will rid the world of this fact. What this means, concretely, will vary across the globe. There are ways of distributing vulnerability, differential forms of allocation that make some populations more subject to arbitrary violence than others. But in that order of things, it would not be possible to maintain that the US has greater security problems than some of the more contested and vulnerable nations and peoples of the world. To be injured means that one has the chance to reflect upon injury, to find out the mechanisms of its distribution, to find out who else suffers from permeable borders, unexpected violence, dispossession, and fear, and in what ways. If national sovereignty is challenged, that does not mean it must be shored up at all costs, if that results in suspending civil liberties and suppressing political dissent. Rather, the dislocation from First World privilege, however temporary, offers a chance to start to imagine a world in which that violence might be minimized, in which an inevitable interdependency becomes acknowledged as the basis for global political community. I confess to not knowing how to theorize that interdependency. I would suggest, however, that both our political and ethical responsibilities are rooted in the recognition that radical forms of self-sufficiency and unbridled sovereignty are, by definition, disrupted by the larger global processes of which they are a part, that no final control can be secured, and that final control is not, cannot be, an ultimate value.

These essays begin the process of that imagining, although there are no grand utopian conclusions here. The first essay begins with the rise of censorship and anti-intellectualism that took hold in the fall of 2001 when anyone who sought to understand the "reasons" for the attack on the United States was regarded as someone who sought to "exonerate" those who conducted that attack. Editorials in the *New York Times* criticized "excuseniks," exploiting the echoes of "peaceniks"—understood as naive and nostalgic political actors rooted in the frameworks of the sixties—and "refuseniks"—those who refused to comply with Soviet forms of censorship and control and often lost employment as a result. If the term was meant to disparage those who cautioned against war, it inadvertently produced the possibility of an identification of war resistors with courageous human rights activists. The effort at disparagement revealed the difficulty of maintaining a consistently negative view of those who sought a historical and political understanding of the events of September 11 much less of those who opposed war against Afghanistan as a legitimate response.

I argue that it is not a vagary of moral relativism to try to understand what might have led to the attacks on the United States. Further, one can—and ought to—abhor the attacks on ethical grounds (and enumerate those grounds), feel a full measure of grief for those losses, but let neither moral outrage nor public mourning become the occasion for the muting of critical discourse and public debate on the meaning of historical events. One might still want to know what brought about these events, want to know how best to address those conditions so that the seeds are not sown for further events of this kind, find sites of intervention, help to plan strategies thoughtfully that will not beckon more violence in the future. One can even experience that abhorrence, mourning, anxiety, and fear, and have all of these emotional dispositions lead to a reflection on how others have suffered arbitrary violence at the hands of the US, but also endeavor to produce another public culture and another public policy in which suffering unexpected violence and loss and reactive aggression are not accepted as the norm of political life.

The second piece, "Violence, Mourning, Politics," takes up a psychoanalytic understanding of loss to see why aggression some- times seems so quickly to follow. The essay pursues the problem of a primary vulnerability to others, one that one cannot will away without ceasing to be human. It suggests as well that contemporary forms of national sovereignty constitute efforts to overcome an impressionability and violability that are ineradicable dimensions of human dependency and sociality. I also consider there how certain forms of grief become nationally recognized and amplified, whereas other losses become unthinkable and ungrievable. I argue that a national melancholia, understood as a disavowed mourning, follows upon the erasure from public representations of the names, images, and narratives of those the US has killed. On the other hand, the US's own losses are consecrated in public obituaries that constitute so many acts of nation-building. Some lives are grievable, and others are not; the differential allocation of grievability that decides what kind of subject is and must be grieved, and which kind of subject must not, operates to produce and maintain certain exclusionary conceptions of who is normatively human: what counts as a livable life and a grievable death?

"Indefinite Detention" considers the political implications of those normative conceptions of the human that produce, through an exclusionary process, a host of "unlivable lives" whose legal and political status is suspended. The prisoners indefinitely detained in Guantanamo Bay are not considered "subjects" protected by international law, are not entitled to regular trials, to lawyers, to due process. The military tribunals that have, at this date, not been used, represent a breach of constitutional law that makes final judgments of life and death into the prerogative of the President. The decision to detain some, if not most, of the 680 inmates currently in Guantanamo is left to "officials" who will decide, on uncertain grounds, whether these individuals present a risk to US security. Bound by no legal guidelines except those fabricated for the occasion, these officials garner sovereign power unto themselves. Whereas Foucault argued that sovereignty and governmentality can and do coexist, the particular form of that coexistence in the contemporary war prison has yet to be charted. Governmentality designates a model for conceptualizing power in its diffuse and multivalent operations, focusing on the management of populations, and operating through state and non-state institutions and discourses. In the current war prison, officials of governmentality wield sovereign power, understood here as a lawless and unaccountable operation of power, once legal rule is effectively suspended and military codes take its place. Once again, a lost or injured sovereignty becomes reanimated through rules that allocate final decisions about life and death to the executive branch or to officials with no elected status and bound by no constitutional constraints.

These prisoners are not considered "prisoners" and receive no protection from international law. Although the US claims that its imprisonment methods are consistent with the Geneva Convention, it does not consider itself bound to those accords, and offers none of the legal rights stipulated by that accord. As a result, the humans who are imprisoned in Guantanamo do not count as human; they are not subjects protected by international law. They are not subjects in any legal or normative sense. The dehumanization effected by "indefinite detention" makes use of an ethnic frame for conceiving who will be human, and who will not. Moreover, the policy of "indefinite detention" produces a sphere of imprisonment and punishment unfettered by any laws except those fabricated by the Department of State. The state itself thus attains a certain "indefinite" power to suspend the law and to fabricate the law, at which point the separation of powers is indefinitely set aside. The Patriot Act constitutes another effort to suspend civil liberties in the name of security, one that I do not consider in these pages, but hope to in a future article. In versions 1 and 2 of the Patriot Act, it is the public intellectual culture that is targeted for control and regulation, overriding long-standing claims to intellectual freedom and freedom of association that have been central to conceptions of democratic political life.

"The Charge of Anti-Semitism: Jews, Israel, and the Risks of Public Critique" considers one effort to quell public criticism and intellectual debate in the context of criticisms of Israeli state and military policy. The remark made by Harvard's President, Lawrence Summers, that to criticize Israel is to engage in "effective" anti-Semitism is critically examined for its failure to distinguish between Jews and Israel, and for the importance of acknowledging publicly those progressive Jewish (Israeli and diasporic) efforts of resistance to the current Israeli state. I consider the consequential implications of his statement, one that expressed sentiments that many people and organizations share, for censoring certain kinds of critical speech by allying those who speak critically with anti-Semitic aims. Given how heinous any identification with anti-Semitism is, especially for progressive Jews who wage their criticisms as Jews, it follows that those who might object to Israeli policy or, indeed, to the doctrine and practice of Zionism, find themselves in the situation of either muting critical speech or braving the unbearable stigma of anti-Semitism by virtue of speaking publicly about their views. This restriction on speaking is enforced through the regulation of psychic and public identifications, specifically, by the threat of having to live in a radically uninhabitable and unacceptable identification with anti-Semitism if one speaks against Israeli policy or, indeed, Israel itself. When the charge of anti-Semitism is used in this way to quell dissent on the matter of Israel, the charge becomes suspect, thereby depriving the charge of its meaning and importance in what surely must remain an active struggle against existing anti-Semitism.

The public sphere is constituted in part by what cannot be said and what cannot be shown. The limits of the sayable, the limits of what can appear, circumscribe the domain in which political speech operates and certain kinds of subjects appear as viable actors. In this instance, the identification of speech that is critical of Israel with anti-Semitism seeks to render it unsayable. It does this through the allocation of stigma, and seeks to preclude from viable discourse criticisms on the structure of the Israeli state, its preconditions of citizenship, its practices of occupation, and its long-standing violence. I argue in favor of the cessation of both Israeli and Palestinian violence, and suggest that opening up the space for a legitimate public debate, free of intimidation, on the political structure of Israel/ Palestine is crucial to that project.

"Precarious Life" approaches the question of a non-violent ethics, one that is based upon an understanding of how easily human life is annulled. Emmanuel Levinas offers a conception of ethics that rests upon an apprehension of the precariousness of life, one that begins with the precarious life of the Other. He makes use of the "face" as a figure that communicates both the precariousness of life and the interdiction on violence. He gives us a way of understanding how aggression is *not* eradicated in an ethics of non-violence; aggression forms the incessant matter for ethical struggles. Levinas considers the fear and anxiety that aggression seeks to quell, but argues that ethics is precisely a struggle to keep fear and anxiety from turning into murderous action. Although his theological view conjures a scene between two humans each of which bears a face that delivers an ethical demand from a seemingly divine source, his view is nevertheless useful for those cultural analyses that seek to understand how best to depict the human, human grief and suffering, and how best to admit the "faces" of those against whom war is waged into public representation.

The Levinasian face is not precisely or exclusively a human face, although it communicates what is human, what is precarious, what is injurable. The media representations of the faces of the "enemy" efface what is most human about the "face" for Levinas. Through a cultural transposition of his philosophy, it is possible to see how dominant forms of representation can and must be disrupted for something about the precariousness of life to be apprehended. This has implications, once again, for the boundaries that constitute what will and will not appear within public life, the limits of a publicly acknowledged field of appearance. Those who remain faceless or whose faces are presented to us as so many symbols of evil, authorize us to become senseless before those lives we have eradicated, and whose grievability is indefinitely postponed. Certain faces must be admitted into public view, must be seen and heard for some keener sense of the value of life, all life, to take hold. So, it is not that mourning is the goal of politics, but that without the capacity to mourn, we lose that keener sense of life we need in order to oppose violence. And though for some, mourning can only be resolved through violence, it seems clear that violence only brings on more loss, and the failure to heed the claim of precarious life only leads, again and again, to the dry grief of an endless political rage. And whereas some forms of public mourning are protracted and ritualized, stoking nationalist fervor, reiterating the conditions of loss and victimization that come to justify a more or less permanent war, not all forms of mourning lead to that conclusion.

Dissent and debate depend upon the inclusion of those who maintain critical views of state policy and civic culture remaining part of a larger public discussion of the value of policies and politics. To charge those who voice critical views with treason, terrorist-sympathizing, anti-Semitism, moral relativism, postmodernism, juvenile behavior, collaboration, anachronistic Leftism, is to seek to destroy the credibility not of the views that are held, but of the persons who hold them. It produces the climate of fear in which to voice a certain view is to risk being branded and shamed with a heinous appellation. To continue to voice one's views under those conditions is not easy, since one must not only discount the truth of the appellation, but brave the stigma that seizes up from the public domain. Dissent is quelled, in part, through threatening the speaking subject with an uninhabitable identification. Because it would be heinous to identify as treasonous, as a collaborator, one fails to speak, or one speaks in throttled ways, in order to sidestep the terrorizing identification that threatens to take hold. This strategy for quelling dissent and limiting the reach of critical debate happens not only through a series of shaming tactics which have a certain psycho-logical terrorization as their effect, but they work as well by producing what will and will not count as a viable speaking subject and a reasonable opinion within the public domain. It is precisely because one does not want to lose one's status as a viable speaking being that one does not say what one thinks. Under social conditions that regulate identifications and the sense of viability to this degree, censorship operates implicitly and forcefully. The line that circumscribes what is speakable and what is livable also functions as an instrument of censorship.

To decide what views will count as reasonable within the public domain, however, is to decide what will and will not count as the public sphere of debate. And if someone holds views that are not in line with the nationalist norm, that person comes to lack credibility as a speaking person, and the media is not open to him or her (though the internet, interestingly, is). The foreclosure of critique empties the public domain of debate and democratic contestation itself, so that debate becomes the exchange of views among the like-minded, and criticism, which ought to be central to any democracy, becomes a fugitive and suspect activity.

Public policy, including foreign policy, often seeks to restrain the public sphere from being open to certain forms of debate and the circulation of media coverage. One way a hegemonic understanding of politics is achieved is through circumscribing what will and will not be admissible as part of the public sphere itself. Without disposing populations in such a way that war seems good and right and true, no war can claim popular consent, and no administration can maintain its popularity. To produce what will constitute the public sphere, however, it is necessary to control the way in which people see, how they hear, what they see. The constraints are not only on content—certain images of dead bodies in Iraq, for instance, are considered unacceptable for public visual consumption—but on what "can" be heard, read, seen, felt, and known. The public sphere is constituted in part by what can appear, and the regulation of the sphere of appearance is one way to establish what will count as reality, and what will not. It is also a way of establishing whose lives can be marked as lives, and whose deaths will count as deaths. Our capacity to feel and to apprehend hangs in the balance. But so, too, does the fate of the reality of certain lives and deaths as well as the ability to think critically and publicly about the effects of war.

Berkeley, California
July, 2003

1

EXPLANATION AND EXONERATION, OR WHAT WE CAN HEAR

Since the events of September 11, we have seen both a rise of anti-intellectualism and a growing acceptance of censorship within the media. This could mean that we have support for these trends within the general population of the United States, but it could also mean that the media function as "public voices" that operate at a distance from their constituency, that both report the "voice" of the government for us, and whose proximity to that voice rests on an alliance or identification with that voice. Setting aside for the moment how the media act upon the public, whether, indeed, they have charged themselves with the task of structuring public sentiment and fidelity, it seems crucial to note that a critical relation to government has been severely, though not fully, suspended, and that the "criticism" or, indeed, independence of the media has been compromised in some unprecedented ways.

Although we have heard, lately, about the abusive treatment of prisoners, and war "mistakes" have been publicly exposed, it seems that neither the justification nor the cause of the war have been the focus of public intellectual attention. Only recently (fall, 2003), have the reasons for waging a preemptive war against Iraq begun to be subjected to public scrutiny. Indeed, thinking too hard about what brought this about has invariably raised fears that to find a set of causes will be to have found a set of excuses. This point was made in print by Michael Walzer, a "just war" proponent, and has worked as an implicit force of censorship in op-ed pages across the country. Similarly, we have heard from Vice-President Richard Cheney and Edward Rothstein of the *New York Times*, among several others, that the time to reassert not only American values but fundamental and absolute values has arrived. Intellectual positions that are considered "relativistic" or "post-" of any kind are considered either complicitous with terrorism or as constituting a "weak link" in the fight against it. The voicing of critical perspectives against the war has become difficult to do, not only because mainstream media enterprises will not publish them (most of them appear in the progressive or alternative print media or on the internet), but because to voice them is to risk hystericization and censorship. In a strong sense, the binarism that Bush proposes in which only two positions are possible—"Either you're with us or you're with the terrorists"— makes it untenable to hold a position in which one opposes both and queries the terms in which the opposition is framed. Moreover, it is the same binarism that returns us to an anachronistic division between "East" and "West" and which, in its sloshy metonymy, returns us to the invidious distinction between civilization (our own) and barbarism (now coded as "Islam" itself). At the beginning of this conflict, to oppose the war meant to some that one somehow felt sympathy with terrorism, or that one saw the terror as justified. But it is surely time to allow an intellectual field to redevelop in which more responsible distinctions might be heard, histories might be recounted in their complexity, and accountability might be understood apart from the claims of vengeance. This would also have to be a field in which the long-range prospects for global cooperation might work as a guide for public reflection and criticism.

The Left's response to the war waged in Afghanistan ran into serious problems, in part because the explanations that the Left has provided to the question "Why do they hate us so much?" were dismissed as so many exonerations of the acts of terror themselves. This does not need to be the case. I think we can see, however, how moralistic anti-intellectual trends coupled with a distrust of the Left as so many self-flagellating First World elites has produced a situation in which our very capacity to think about the grounds and causes of the current global conflict is considered impermissible. The cry that "there is no excuse for September 11" has become a means by which to stifle any serious public discussion of how US foreign policy has helped to create a world in which such acts of terror are possible. We see this most dramatically in the suspension of any attempt to offer balanced reporting on the international conflict, the refusal to include important critiques of the US military effort by Arundhati Roy[1] and Noam Chomsky, for instance, within the mainstream US press. This takes place in tandem with the unprecedented suspension of civil liberties for illegal immigrants and suspected terrorists, and the use of the flag as an ambiguous sign of solidarity with those lost on September 11 and with the current war, as if the sympathy with the one translates, in a single symbolic stroke, into support for the latter. The raw public mockery of the peace movement, and the characterization of anti-war demonstrations as anachronistic or nostalgic, work to produce a consensus of public opinion that profoundly marginalizes anti-war sentiment and analysis, putting into question in a very strong way the very value of dissent as part of contemporary US democratic culture.

The articulation of this hegemony takes place in part through producing a consensus on what certain terms will mean, how they can be used, and what lines of solidarity are implicitly drawn through this use. We reserve "acts of terror" for events such as the September 11 attacks on the United States, distinguishing these acts of violence from those that might be justified through foreign policy decisions or public declarations of war. On the other hand, these terrorist acts were construed as "declarations of war" by the Bush administration, which then positioned the military response as a justified act of self-defense. In the meantime, there remains ever-increasing ambiguity introduced by the very use of the term "terrorist," which is then exploited by various powers at war with independence movements of various kinds. The term "terrorist" is used, for instance, by the Israeli state to describe any and all Palestinian acts of resistance, but none of its own practices of state violence. The term is also used by Putin to describe the Chechen struggle for independence, which then casts its own acts of violence against this province as justified acts of national self-defense. The United States, by using the term, positions itself exclusively as the sudden and indisputable victim of violence, even though there is no doubt that it did suffer violence. But it is one matter to suffer violence and quite another to use that fact to ground a framework in which one's injury authorizes limitless aggression against targets that may or may not be related to the sources of one's own suffering.

The point I would like to underscore here is that a frame for understanding violence emerges in tandem with the experience, and that the frame works both to preclude certain kinds of questions, certain kinds of historical inquiries, and to function as a moral justification for retaliation. It seems crucial to attend to this frame, since it decides, in a forceful way, *what we can hear*, whether a view will be taken as explanation or as exoneration, whether we can hear the difference, and abide by it.

There is as well a narrative dimension to this explanatory framework. In the United States, we begin the story by invoking a first-person narrative point of view, and telling what happened on September 11. It is that date and the unexpected and fully terrible experience of violence that propels the narrative. If someone tries to start the story earlier, there are only a few narrative options. We can narrate, for instance, what Mohammed Atta's family life was like, whether he was teased for looking like a girl, where he congregated in Hamburg, and what led, psychologically, to the moment in which he piloted the plane into the World Trade Center. Or what was bin Laden's break from his family, and why is he so angry? That kind of story is interesting to a degree, because it suggests that there is a personal pathology at work. It works as a plausible and engaging narrative in part because it resituates agency in terms of a subject, something we can understand, something that accords with our idea of personal responsibility, or with the theory of charismatic leadership that was popularized with Mussolini and Hitler in World War II.

This is doubtless easier to hear than that a network of individuals dispersed across the globe conjured and implemented this action in various ways. If there is a network, there must be a leader, a subject who is finally responsible for what others do. Perhaps we can hear, in a limited way, about the way in which the al-Qaeda group makes use of Islamic doctrine, and we want to know, to shore up our liberal framework, that they do not represent the religion of Islam, and that the vast majority of Muslims do not condone them. Al-Qaeda can be "the subject," but do we ask where this comes from? Isolating the individuals involved absolves us of the necessity of coming up with a broader explanation for events. Though we are perhaps perplexed

by why there is not a greater public repudiation by Muslim leaders
(though many organizations have done that), we cannot quite understand why it might be difficult for Muslim leaders to join publicly
with the United States on this issue even as they condemn quite
clearly the acts of violence.

Our own acts of violence do not receive graphic coverage in the
press, and so they remain acts that are justified in the name of self-
defense, but by a noble cause, namely, the rooting out of terrorism.
At one point during the war against Afghanistan, it was reported that
the Northern Alliance may have slaughtered a village: Was this to be
investigated and, if confirmed, prosecuted as a war crime? When a
bleeding child or dead body on Afghan soil emerges in the press
coverage, it is not relayed as part of the horror of war, but only in the
service of a criticism of the military's capacity to aim its bombs right.
We castigate ourselves for not aiming better, as if the end goal is to
aim right. We do not, however, take the sign of destroyed life and
decimated peoples as something for which we are responsible, or
indeed understand how that decimation works to confirm the United
States as performing atrocities. Our own acts are not considered
terrorist. And there is no history of acts that is relevant to the self-
understanding we form in the light of these terrible events. There is
no relevant prehistory to the events of September 11, since to begin
to tell the story a different way, to ask how things came to this, is
already to complicate the question of agency which, no doubt, leads
to the fear of moral equivocation. In order to condemn these acts
as inexcusable, absolutely wrong, in order to sustain the affective
structure in which we are, on the one hand, victimized and, on the
other, engaged in a righteous cause of rooting out terror, we have to
begin the story with the experience of violence we suffered.

We have to shore up the first-person point of view, and preclude
from the telling accounts that might involve a decentering of the

narrative "I" within the international political domain. This decentering is experienced as part of the wound that we have suffered, though, so we cannot inhabit that position. This decentering is precisely what we seek to rectify through a recentering. A narrative form emerges to compensate for the enormous narcissistic wound opened up by the public display of our physical vulnerability. Our response, accordingly, is not to enter into international coalitions where we understand ourselves to be working with institutionally established routes of consensus-building. We relegate the United Nations to a second-order deliberative body, and insist instead on American unilateralism. And subsequently we ask, Who is with us? Who is against us? As a result, we respond to the exposure of vulnerability with an assertion of US "leadership," showing once again the contempt we have for international coalitions that are not built and led by us. Such coalitions do not conflict with US supremacy, but confirm it, stoke it, insist upon it, with long-term implications for the future shape and possibility of global cooperation.

Perhaps the question cannot be heard at all, but I would still like to ask: Can we find another meaning, and another possibility, for the decentering of the first-person narrative within the global framework? I do not mean that the story of being attacked should not be told. I do not mean that the story that begins with September 11 should not be told. These stories have to be told, and they are being told, despite the enormous trauma that undermines narrative capacity in these instances. But if we are to come to understand ourselves as global actors, and acting within a historically established field, and one that has other actions in play, we will need to emerge from the narrative perspective of US unilateralism and, as it were, its defensive structures, to consider the ways in which our lives are profoundly implicated in the lives of others. My friends on the Left joke about having lost their First World complacency. Yes, this is true. But do we now seek to restore it as a way of healing from this wound? Or do we allow the challenge to First World complacency to stand and begin to build a different politics on its basis?

My sense is that being open to the explanations, poorly circulated as they are in the United States, that might help us take stock of how the world has come to take this form will involve us in a different order of responsibility. The ability to narrate ourselves not from the first person alone, but from, say, the position of the third, or to receive an account delivered in the second, can actually work to expand our understanding of the forms that global power has taken. But instead of remaining open to a consequential decentering of First Worldism, we tend to dismiss any effort at explanation, as if to explain these events would accord them rationality, as if to explain these events would involve us in a sympathetic identification with the oppressor, as if to understand these events would involve building a justificatory framework for them. Our fear of understanding a point of view belies a deeper fear that we shall be taken up by it, find it is contagious, become infected in a morally perilous way by the thinking of the presumed enemy. But why do we assume this? We claim to have gone to war in order to "root out" the sources of terror, according to Bush, but do we think that finding the individuals responsible for the attacks on the United States will constitute having gotten to the root? Do we not imagine that the invasion of a sovereign country with a substantial Muslim population, supporting the military regime in Pakistan that actively and violently suppresses free speech, obliterating lives and villages and homes and hospitals, will not foster more adamant and widely disseminated anti-American sentiment and political organizing? Are we not, strategically speaking, interested in ameliorating this violence? Are we not, ethically speaking, obligated to stop its further dissemination, to consider our role in instigating it, and to foment and cultivate another sense of a culturally and religiously diverse global political culture?

Part of the problem the United States is up against is that liberals quietly lined up behind the war effort, and supplied in part the rationale that keeps US state violence from being labeled as terrorist. It is not only the conservative Republicans who did not want to hear about "causes." The "just war" liberal Left made plain that it did not want to hear from "excuseniks." This coinage, rehabilitating the Cold War rhetoric about Soviet Russia, suggests that those who seek to understand how the global map arrived at this juncture through asking how, in part, the United States has contributed to the making of this map, are themselves, through the style of their inquiry, and the shape of their questions, complicitous with an assumed enemy. But to ask how certain political and social actions come into being, such as the recent terrorist attacks on the United States, and even to identify a set of causes, is not the same as locating the source of responsibility for these actions or, indeed, paralyzing our capacity to make ethical judgments on what is right or wrong.

No doubt there are forms of Left analysis that say simply that the United States has reaped what it has sown. Or they say that the United States has brought this state of events on itself. These are, as closed explanations, simply other ways of asserting US priority and encoding US omnipotence. These are also explanations that assume that these actions originate in a single subject, that the subject is not what it appears to be, that it is the United States that occupies the site of that subject, and that no other subjects exist or, if they exist, their agency is subordinated to our own. In other words, political paranoia of this kind is just another articulation of US supremacy. Paranoia is fed by the fantasy of omnipotence, and we see this evidenced in some of the more extreme explanations of this kind, that is, the attacks on September 11 were masterminded by the CIA or Mossad, the Israeli secret police. It is clear, though, that bin Laden did apprentice to the CIA and that the United States supported the Taliban since the 1990s, when it was deemed strategically useful. These links are not precisely causal explanations, but they are part of an explanatory framework. They do not translate into the notion that the United States performed these acts, but one can see how the connection becomes the occasion for the causal reduction, and a certain paranoia amplifies itself by seizing upon part of a broader explanatory picture.

What is generally heard when these opinions are expressed is that the United States is the culpable agent, that it is, effectively, the author of these events, and that the United States is solely responsible for this global outcome. This kind of reasoning is unacceptable to the press, and to the public in general, because it seems to blame the victim in this instance. But is this the only way to hear this point of view? And is this the only form this point of view takes? It seems that being most precise about this point, and publicizing it where one can, will be crucial for any effort by the Left to offer an anti-war view-point within contemporary public discourse.

If we believe that to think radically about the formation of the current situation is to exculpate those who committed acts of violence, we shall freeze our thinking in the name of a questionable morality. But if we paralyze our thinking in this way, we shall fail morality in a different way. We shall fail to take collective respon-sibility for a thorough understanding of the history that brings us to this juncture. We shall thereby deprive ourselves of the very critical and historical resources we need to imagine and practice another future, one that will move beyond the current cycle of revenge.

When President Arroyo of the Philippines on October 29, 2001, remarks that "the best breeding ground [for terrorism] is poverty," or Arundhati Roy claims that bin Laden has been "sculpted from the spare rib of a world laid waste by America's foreign policy," something less than a strictly causal explanation is being offered. A "breeding ground" does not necessarily breed, but it can. And the "spare rib" that is said to emerge from a world laid waste by US foreign policy has, by definition, emerged in a strange and alchemical fashion. It is from waste that this rib is formed, as if the bone belongs to the dead, or is itself the animation of skeletal remains. This form of alchemical making is not the same as God creating Eve from the rib of Adam, life generating life, but has to be understood as death generating death through a means that is figural, not precisely causal. Indeed, both of them make use of figures—grounds and bones—to bespeak a kind of generation that precedes and exceeds a strictly causal frame. Both of them are pointing to conditions, not causes. A condition of terrorism can be necessary or sufficient. If it is necessary, it is a state of affairs without which terrorism cannot take hold, one that terrorism absolutely requires. If it is sufficient, its presence is enough for terrorism to take place. Conditions do not "act" in the way that individual agents do, but no agent acts without them. They are presupposed in what we do, but it would be a mistake to personify them as if they acted in the place of us. Thus, we can say, and ought to, that US imperialism is a necessary condition for the attacks on the United States, that these attacks would be impossible without the horizon of imperialism within which they occur. But to understand how US imperialism figures here, we have to understand not only how it is experienced by those who understand themselves as its victims, but how it enters into their own formation as acting and deliberating subjects.

This is the beginning of another kind of account. And this seems to be, for instance, what Mary Kaldor in *The Nation* points to when she claims that "in many of the areas where war takes place and where extreme networks pick up new recruits, becoming a criminal or joining a paramilitary group is literally the only opportunity for unemployed young men lacking formal education."[2] What effect did the killing of an estimated 200,000 Iraqi citizens, including tens of thousands of children, and the subsequent starvation of Muslim populations, predicted by Concern, a hunger relief organization, to reach six million by the year's end, have on Muslim views of the United States? Is a Muslim life as valuable as legibly First World lives? Are the Palestinians yet accorded the status of "human" in US policy and press coverage? Will those hundreds of thousands of Muslim lives lost in the last decades of strife ever receive the equivalent to the paragraph-long obituaries in the *New York Times* that seek to humanize—often through nationalist and familial framing devices— those Americans who have been violently killed? Is our capacity to mourn in global dimensions foreclosed precisely by the failure to conceive of Muslim and Arab lives *as lives*?

Former New York City mayor Rudolph Giuliani's response to Saudi Prince Alwaleed bin Talal's remarks on October 11 in New York raises this question of the acceptability of critical discourse emphatically. The prince came with a check for $10 million in hand for the World Trade Center relief effort and expressed at the same time horror and moral condemnation of the attacks on the World Trade Center, asking that "the United States take a more balanced stand toward the Palestinian cause." Forbes.com reported Giuliani's refusal of the check in this way: While in New York, Alwaleed said, "Our Palestinian brethren continue to be slaughtered at the hands of Israelis while the world turns the other cheek." At a news conference, Giuliani said, "Not only are those statements wrong, they are part of the problem. There is no moral equivalent to this attack. There is no justification for it .... The people who did it lost any right to ask for justification for it when they slaughtered four or five thousand innocent people, and to suggest that there is any justification for it only invites this happening in the future."[3] The Saudi prince, the sixth richest man in the world, did say he condemned terrorism, and he expressed his condolences for the more than 3,000 people killed when hijacked jets slammed into the World Trade Center and the Pentagon.

In a television report that same day, Giuliani announced that Alwaleed's views were "absolutely wrong." I would suggest that it was not possible to hear both of these views at the same time because the framework for hearing presumes that the one view nullifies the other, so either the claim of grief or the offer of help is considered disingenuous. Or, what is heard is that the failure of the United States to offer a balanced approach to the Palestinian cause provides a justification for the attacks. Alwaleed had been clear, and was subsequently clear in a *New York Times* editorial, that he did not think that the US policy failure, which he deems true, to honor the Palestinian cause, justifies the attacks. But he did think that long-term US–Arab relations would be improved were the United States to develop a more balanced approach. It makes sense to assume that bettering those relations might well lead to less conducive grounds for Islamic extremism. The Bush administration itself, in its own way, attests to this belief by pursuing the possibility of a Palestinian state. But here the two views could not be heard together, and it has to do with the utterability of the word "slaughter" in the context of saying that Israelis have slaughtered and do slaughter Palestinians, in large numbers.

Like "terrorist," "slaughter" is a word that, within the hegemonic grammar, should be reserved for unjustified acts of violence against First World nations, if I understand the grammar correctly. Giuliani hears this as a discourse of justification, since he believes that slaughter justifies military self-defense. He calls the statements "absolutely untrue," I presume, not because he disputes that there have been deaths on the Palestinian side, and that the Israelis are responsible for them, but because "slaughter" as the name for those deaths implies an equivalence with the deaths of the World Trade Center victims. It seems, though, that we are not supposed to say that both groups of people have been "slaughtered" since that implies a "moral equivalence," meaning, I suppose, that the slaughtering of one group is as bad as the slaughtering of the next, and that both, according to his framework, would be entitled to self-defense as a result.

Although the prince subsequently undermined his credibility when he betrayed anti-Semitic beliefs, claiming that "Jewish pressure" was behind Giuliani's refusal of the check, he nevertheless initiated an utterance and a formulation that had value on its own. Why is it that Israeli and Palestinian deaths are not viewed as equally horrible? To what extent has the very refusal to apprehend Palestinian deaths as "slaughter" produced an immeasurable rage on the part of Arabs who seek some legitimate recognition and resolution for this continuing state of violence? One does not need to enter into the dreary business of quantifying and comparing oppressions to understand what the prince meant to say, and subsequently said, namely, that the United States needs to think about how its own political investments and practices help to create a world of enormous rage and violence. This view does not imply that the acts of violence perpetrated on September 11 were the "fault" of the United States, nor does it does exonerate those who committed them. One way to read what the prince had to say was that the acts of terror were unequivocally wrong, and that the United States might also be able to intervene more productively in global politics to produce conditions in which this response to US imperialism becomes less likely. This is not the same as holding the United States exclusively responsible for the violence done within its borders, but it does ask the United States to assume a different kind of responsibility for producing more egalitarian global conditions for equality, sovereignty, and the egalitarian redistribution of resources.

Similarly, the *New York Times* describes Arundhati Roy's critique of US imperialism as "anti-US," implying that any position that seeks to critically reevaluate US foreign policy in light of September 11 and the ensuing war is anti-US or, indeed, complicitous with the presumed enemy.[4] This is tantamount to the suppression of dissent, and the nationalist refusal to consider the merits of criticisms developed from other parts of the globe. The treatment is unfair. Roy's condemnation of bin Laden is clear, but she is willing to ask how he was formed. To condemn the violence and to ask how it came about are surely two separate issues, but they need to be examined in tandem, held in juxtaposition, reconciled within a broader analysis. Under contemporary strictures on public discourse, however, this kind of dual thinking cannot be heard: it is dismissed as contradictory or disingenuous, and Roy herself is treated as a diva or a cult figure, rather than listened to as a political critic with a wide moral compass.

So, is there a way, in Roy's terms, to understand bin Laden as "born" from the rib of US imperialism (allowing that he is born from several possible historical sources, one of which is, crucially, US imperialism), without claiming that US imperialism is solely responsible for his actions, or those of his ostensible network? To answer this question, we need to distinguish, provisionally, between individual and collective responsibility. But, then we need to situate individual responsibility in light of its collective conditions. Those who commit acts of violence are surely responsible for them; they are not dupes or mechanisms of an impersonal social force, but agents with responsibility. On the other hand, these individuals are formed, and we would be making a mistake if we reduced their actions to purely self-generated acts of will or symptoms of individual pathology or "evil." Both the discourse of individualism and of moralism (understood as the moment in which morality exhausts itself in public acts of denunciation) assume that the individual is the first link in a causal chain that forms the meaning of accountability. But to take the self-generated acts of the individual as our point of departure in moral reasoning is precisely to foreclose the possibility of questioning what kind of world gives rise to such individuals. And what is this process of "giving rise"? What social conditions help to form the very ways that choice and deliberation proceed? Where and how can such subject formations be contravened? How is it that radical violence becomes an option, comes to appear as the only viable option for some, under some global conditions? Against what conditions of violation do they respond? And with what resources?

To ask these questions is not to say that the conditions are at fault rather than the individual. It is, rather, to rethink the relation between conditions and acts. Our acts are not self-generated, but conditioned. We are at once acted upon and acting, and our "responsibility" lies in the juncture between the two. What can I do with the conditions that form me? What do they constrain me to do? What can I do to transform them? Being acted upon is not fully continuous with acting, and in this way the forces that act upon us are not finally responsible for what we do. In a certain way, and paradoxically, our responsibility is heightened once we have been subjected to the violence of others. We are acted upon, violently, and it appears that our capacity to set our own course at such instances is fully undermined. Only once we have suffered that violence are we compelled, ethically, to ask how we will respond to violent injury. What role will we assume in the historical relay of violence, who will we become in the response, and will we be furthering or impeding violence by virtue of the response that we make? To respond to violence with violence may well seem "justified," but is it finally a responsible solution? Similarly, moralistic denunciation provides immediate gratification, and even has the effect of temporarily cleansing the speaker of all proximity to guilt through the act of self-righteous denunciation itself. But is this the same as responsibility, understood as taking stock of our world, and participating in its social transformation in such a way that non-violent, cooperative, egalitarian international relations remain the guiding ideal?

We ask these latter questions not to exonerate the individuals who commit violence, but to take a different sort of responsibility for the global conditions of justice. As a result, it made sense after 9/11 to follow two courses of action at once: to find those who planned and implemented the violence and to hold them accountable according to international war crimes standards and in international courts of law, regardless of our skepticism about such institutions (skepticism can furnish grounds for reform or for the making of new law or new institutions for implementing law). In pursuing a wayward military solution, the United States perpetrates and displays its own violence, offering a breeding ground for new waves of young Muslims to join terrorist organizations. This is poor thinking, strategically and morally. Ignoring its image as the hated enemy for many in the region, the United States has effectively responded to the violence done against it by consolidating its reputation as a militaristic power with no respect for lives outside of the First World. That we now respond with more violence is taken as "further proof" that the United States has violent and anti-sovereign designs on the region. To remember the lessons of Aeschylus, and to refuse this cycle of revenge in the name of justice, means not only to seek legal redress for wrongs done, but to take stock of how the world has become formed in this way precisely in order to form it anew, and in the direction of non-violence.

Our collective responsibility not merely as a nation, but as part of an international community based on a commitment to equality and non-violent cooperation, requires that we ask how these conditions came about, and endeavor to re-create social and political conditions on more sustaining grounds. This means, in part, hearing beyond what we are able to hear. And it means as well being open to narration that decenters us from our supremacy, in both its right- and left-wing forms. Can we hear that there were precedents for these events and even know that it is urgent to know and learn from these precedents as we seek to stop them from operating in the present, at the same time as we insist that these precedents do not "justify" the recent violent events? If the events are not understandable without that history, that does not mean that the historical understanding furnishes a moral justification for the events themselves. Only then do we reach the disposition to get to the "root" of violence, and begin to offer another vision of the future than that which perpetuates violence in the name of denying it, offering instead names for things that restrain us from thinking and acting radically and well about global options.

2

VIOLENCE, MOURNING, POLITICS

I propose to consider a dimension of political life that has to do with our exposure to violence and our complicity in it, with our vulnerability to loss and the task of mourning that follows, and with finding a basis for community in these conditions. We cannot precisely "argue against" these dimensions of human vulnerability, inasmuch as they function, in effect, as the limits of the arguable, even perhaps as the fecundity of the inarguable. It is not that my thesis survives any argument against it: surely there are various ways of regarding corporeal vulnerability and the task of mourning, and various ways of figuring these conditions within the sphere of politics. But if the opposition is to vulnerability and the task of mourning itself, regardless of its formulation, then it is probably best not to regard this opposition primarily as an "argument." Indeed, if there were no opposition to this thesis, then there would be no reason to write this essay. And, if the opposition to this thesis were not consequential, there would be no political reason for reimagining the possibility of community on the basis of vulnerability and loss.

Perhaps, then, it should come as no surprise that I propose to start, and to end, with the question of the human (as if there were any other way for us to start or end!). We start here not because there is a human condition that is universally shared— this is surely not yet the case. The question that preoccupies me in the light of recent global violence is, Who counts as human? Whose lives count as lives? And, finally, What *makes for a grievable life*? Despite our differences in location and history, my guess is that it is possible to appeal to a "we," for all of us have some notion of what it is to have lost somebody. Loss has made a tenuous "we" of us all. And if we have lost, then it follows that we have had, that we have desired and loved, that we have struggled to find the conditions for our desire. We have all lost in recent decades from AIDS, but there are other losses that afflict us, from illness and from global conflict; and there is the fact as well that women and minorities, including sexual minorities, are, as a community, subjected to violence, exposed to its possibility, if not its realization. This means that each of us is constituted politically in part by virtue of the social vulnerability of our bodies—as a site of desire and physical vulnerability, as a site of a publicity at once assertive and exposed. Loss and vulnerability seem to follow from our being socially constituted bodies, attached to others, at risk of losing those attachments, exposed to others, at risk of violence by virtue of that exposure.

I am not sure I know when mourning is successful, or when one has fully mourned another human being. Freud changed his mind on this subject: he suggested that successful mourning meant being able to exchange one object for another;[1] he later claimed that incorporation, originally associated with melancholia, was essential to the task of mourning.[2] Freud's early hope that an attachment might be withdrawn and then given anew implied a certain interchangeability of objects as a sign of hopefulness, as if the prospect of entering life anew made use of a kind of promiscuity of libidinal aim.[3] That might be true, but I do not think that successful grieving implies that one has forgotten another person or that something else has come along to take its place, as if full substitutability were something for which we might strive.

Perhaps, rather, one mourns when one accepts that by the loss one undergoes one will be changed, possibly for ever. Perhaps mourning has to do with agreeing to undergo a transformation (perhaps one should say *submitting* to a transformation) the full result of which one cannot know in advance. There is losing, as we know, but there is also the transformative effect of loss, and this latter cannot be charted or planned. One can try to choose it, but it may be that this experience of transformation deconstitutes choice at some level. I do not think, for instance, that one can invoke the Protestant ethic when it comes to loss. One cannot say, "Oh, I'll go through loss this way, and that will be the result, and I'll apply myself to the task, and I'll endeavor to achieve the resolution of grief that is before me." I think one is hit by waves, and that one starts out the day with an aim, a project, a plan, and finds oneself foiled. One finds oneself fallen. One is exhausted but does not know why. Something is larger than one's own deliberate plan, one's own project, one's own knowing and choosing.

Something takes hold of you: where does it come from? What sense does it make? What claims us at such moments, such that we are not the masters of ourselves? To what are we tied? And by what are we seized? Freud reminded us that when we lose someone, we do not always know what it is *in* that person that has been lost.[4] So when one loses, one is also faced with something enigmatic: something is hiding in the loss, something is lost within the recesses of loss. If mourning involves knowing what one has lost (and melancholia originally meant, to a certain extent, not knowing), then mourning would be maintained by its enigmatic dimension, by the experience of not knowing incited by losing what we cannot fully fathom.

When we lose certain people, or when we are dispossessed from a place, or a community, we may simply feel that we are undergoing something temporary, that mourning will be over and some restoration of prior order will be achieved. But maybe when we undergo what we do, something about who we are is revealed, something that delineates the ties we have to others, that shows us that these ties constitute what we are, ties or bonds that compose us. It is not as if an "I" exists independently over here and then simply loses a "you" over there, especially if the attachment to "you" is part of what composes who "I" am. If I lose you, under these conditions, then I not only mourn the loss, but I become inscrutable to myself. Who "am" I, without you? When we lose some of these ties by which we are constituted, we do not know who we are or what to do. On one level, I think I have lost "you" only to discover that "I" have gone missing as well. At another level, perhaps what I have lost "in" you, that for which I have no ready vocabulary, is a relationality that is composed neither exclusively of myself nor you, but is to be conceived as *the tie* by which those terms are differentiated and related.

Many people think that grief is privatizing, that it returns us to a solitary situation and is, in that sense, depoliticizing. But I think it furnishes a sense of political community of a complex order, and it does this first of all by bringing to the fore the relational ties that have implications for theorizing fundamental dependency and ethical responsibility. If my fate is not originally or finally separable from yours, then the "we" is traversed by a relationality that we cannot easily argue against; or, rather, we can argue against it, but we would be denying something fundamental about the social conditions of our very formation.

A consequential grammatical quandary follows. In the effort to explain these relations, I might be said to "have" them, but what does "having" imply? I might sit back and try to enumerate them to you. I might explain what this friendship means, what that lover meant or means to me. I would be constituting myself in such an instance as a detached narrator of my relations. Dramatizing my detachment, I might perhaps only be showing that the form of attachment I am demonstrating is trying to minimize its own relationality, is invoking it as an option, as something that does not touch on the question of what sustains me fundamentally.

What grief displays, in contrast, is the thrall in which our relations with others hold us, in ways that we cannot always recount or explain, in ways that often interrupt the self-conscious account of ourselves we might try to provide, in ways that challenge the very notion of ourselves as autonomous and in control. I might try to tell a story here about what I am feeling, but it would have to be a story in which the very "I" who seeks to tell the story is stopped in the midst of the telling; the very "I" is called into question by its relation to the Other, a relation that does not precisely reduce me to speechlessness, but does nevertheless clutter my speech with signs of its undoing. I tell a story about the relations I choose, only to expose, somewhere along the way, the way I am gripped and undone by these very relations. My narrative falters, as it must.

Let's face it. We're undone by each other. And if we're not, we're missing something.

This seems so clearly the case with grief, but it can be so only because it was already the case with desire. One does not always stay intact. One may want to, or manage to for a while, but despite one's best efforts, one is undone, in the face of the other, by the touch, by the scent, by the feel, by the prospect of the touch, by the memory of the feel. And so, when we speak about "my sexuality" or "my gender," as we do and as we must, we nevertheless mean something complicated that is partially concealed by our usage. As a mode of relation, neither gender nor sexuality is precisely a possession, but, rather, is a mode of being dispossessed, a way of being *for* another or *by virtue of* another. It won't even do to say that I am promoting a relational view of the self over an autonomous one or trying to redescribe autonomy in terms of relationality. Despite my affinity for the term relationality, we may need other language to approach the issue that concerns us, a way of thinking about how we are not only constituted by our relations but also dispossessed by them as well.

We tend to narrate the history of the feminist and lesbian/gay movement, for instance, in such a way that ecstasy figured prominently in the sixties and seventies and midway through the eighties. But maybe ecstasy is more persistent than that; maybe it is with us all along. To be ec-static means, literally, to be outside oneself, and thus can have several meanings: to be transported beyond oneself by a passion, but also to be *beside oneself* with rage or grief. I think that if I can still address a "we," or include myself within its terms, I am speaking to those of us who are living in certain ways *beside ourselves*, whether in sexual passion, or emotional grief, or political rage.

I am arguing, if I am "arguing" at all, that we have an interesting political predicament; most of the time when we hear about "rights," we understand them as pertaining to individuals. When we argue for protection against discrimination, we argue as a group or a class. And in that language and in that context, we have to present ourselves as bounded beings—distinct, recognizable, delineated, subjects before the law, a community defined by some shared features. Indeed, we must be able to use that language to secure legal protections and entitlements. But perhaps we make a mistake if we take the definitions of who we are, legally, to be adequate descriptions of what we are about. Although this language may well establish our legitimacy within a legal framework ensconced in liberal versions of human ontology, it does not do justice to passion and grief and rage, all of which tear us from ourselves, bind us to others, transport us, undo us, implicate us in lives that are not are own, irreversibly, if not fatally.

It is not easy to understand how a political community is wrought from such ties. One speaks, and one speaks for another, to another, and yet there is no way to collapse the distinction between the Other and oneself. When we say "we" we do nothing more than designate this very problematic. We do not solve it. And perhaps it is, and ought to be, insoluble. This disposition of ourselves outside ourselves seems to follow from bodily life, from its vulnerability and its exposure.

At the same time, essential to so many political movements is the claim of bodily integrity and self-determination. It is important to claim that our bodies are in a sense *our own* and that we are entitled to claim rights of autonomy over our bodies. This assertion is as true for lesbian and gay rights claims to sexual freedom as it is for transsexual and transgender claims to self-determination, as it is to intersex claims to be free of coerced medical and psychiatric interventions. It is as true for all claims to be free from racist attacks, physical and verbal, as it is for feminism's claim to reproductive freedom, and as it surely is for those whose bodies labor under duress, economic and political, under conditions of colonization and occupation. It is difficult, if not impossible, to make these claims without recourse to autonomy. I am not suggesting that we cease to make these claims. We have to, we must. I also do not wish to imply that we have to make these claims reluctantly or strategically. Defined within the broadest possible compass, they are part of any normative aspiration of a movement that seeks to maximize the protection and the freedoms of sexual and gender minorities, of women, and of racial and ethnic minorities, especially as they cut across all the other categories.

But is there another normative aspiration that we must also seek to articulate and to defend? Is there a way in which the place of the body, and the way in which it disposes us outside ourselves or sets us beside ourselves, opens up another kind of normative aspiration within the field of politics?

The body implies mortality, vulnerability, agency: the skin and the flesh expose us to the gaze of others, but also to touch, and to violence, and bodies put us at risk of becoming the agency and instrument of all these as well. Although we struggle for rights over our own bodies, the very bodies for which we struggle are not quite ever only our own. The body has its invariably public dimension. Constituted as a social phenomenon in the public sphere, my body is and is not mine. Given over from the start to the world of others, it bears their imprint, is formed within the crucible of social life; only later, and with some uncertainty, do I lay claim to my body as my own, if, in fact, I ever do. Indeed, if I deny that prior to the formation of my "will," my body related me to others whom I did not choose to have in proximity to myself, if I build a notion of "autonomy" on the basis of the denial of this sphere of a primary and unwilled physical proximity with others, then am I denying the social conditions of my embodiment in the name of autonomy?

At one level, this situation is literally familiar: there is bound to be some experience of humiliation for adults, who think that they are exercising judgment in matters of love, to reflect upon the fact that, as infants and young children, they loved their parents or other primary others in absolute and uncritical ways—and that something of that pattern lives on in their adult relationships. I may wish to reconstitute my "self" as if it were there all along, a tacit ego with acumen from the start; but to do so would be to deny the various forms of rapture and subjection that formed the condition of my emergence as an individuated being and that continue to haunt my adult sense of self with whatever anxiety and longing I may now feel. Individuation is an accomplishment, not a presupposition, and certainly no guarantee.

Is there a reason to apprehend and affirm this condition of my formation within the sphere of politics, a sphere monopolized by adults? If I am struggling for autonomy, do I not need to be struggling for something else as well, a conception of myself as invariably in community, impressed upon by others, impinging upon them as well, and in ways that are not fully in my control or clearly predictable?

Is there a way that we might struggle for autonomy in many spheres, yet also consider the demands that are imposed upon us by living in a world of beings who are, by definition, physically dependent on one another, physically vulnerable to one another? Is this not another way of imagining community, one in which we are alike only in having this condition separately and so having in common a condition that cannot be thought without difference? This way of imagining community affirms relationality not only as a descriptive or historical fact of our formation, but also as an ongoing normative dimension of our social and political lives, one in which we are compelled to take stock of our interdependence. According to this latter view, it would become incumbent on us to consider the place of violence in any such relation, for violence is, always, an exploitation of that primary tie, that primary way in which we are, as bodies, outside ourselves and for one another.

We are something other than "autonomous" in such a condition, but that does not mean that we are merged or without boundaries. It does mean, however, that when we think about who we "are" and seek to represent ourselves, we cannot represent ourselves as merely bounded beings, for the primary others who are past for me not only live on in the fiber of the boundary that contains me (one meaning of "incorporation"), but they also haunt the way I am, as it were, periodically undone and open to becoming unbounded.

Let us return to the issue of grief, to the moments in which one undergoes something outside one's control and finds that one is beside oneself, not at one with oneself. Perhaps we can say that grief contains the possibility of apprehending a mode of dispossession that is fundamental to who I am. This possibility does not dispute the fact of my autonomy, but it does qualify that claim through recourse to the fundamental sociality of embodied life, the ways in which we are, from the start and by virtue of being a bodily being, already given over, beyond ourselves, implicated in lives that are not our own. If I do not always know what seizes me on such occasions, and if I do not always know what it is *in* another person that I have lost, it may be that this sphere of dispossession is precisely the one that exposes my unknowingness, the unconscious imprint of my primary sociality. Can this insight lead to a normative reorientation for politics? Can this situation of mourning—one that is so dramatic for those in social movements who have undergone innumerable losses—supply a perspective by which to begin to apprehend the contemporary global situation?

Mourning, fear, anxiety, rage. In the United States, we have been surrounded with violence, having perpetrated it and perpetrating it still, having suffered it, living in fear of it, planning more of it, if not an open future of infinite war in the name of a "war on terrorism." Violence is surely a touch of the worst order, a way a primary human vulnerability to other humans is exposed in its most terrifying way, a way in which we are given over, without control, to the will of another, a way in which life itself can be expunged by the willful action of another. To the extent that we commit violence, we are acting on another, putting the other at risk, causing the other damage, threatening to expunge the other. In a way, we all live with this particular vulnerability, a vulnerability to the other that is part of bodily life, a vulnerability to a sudden address from elsewhere that we cannot preempt. This vulnerability, however, becomes highly exacerbated under certain social and political conditions, especially those in which violence is a way of life and the means to secure self-defense are limited.

Mindfulness of this vulnerability can become the basis of claims for non-military political solutions, just as denial of this vulnerability through a fantasy of mastery (an institutionalized fantasy of mastery) can fuel the instruments of war. We cannot, however, will away this vulnerability. We must attend to it, even abide by it, as we begin to think about what politics might be implied by staying with the thought of corporeal vulnerability itself, a situation in which we can be vanquished or lose others. Is there something to be learned about the geopolitical distribution of corporeal vulnerability from our own brief and devastating exposure to this condition?

I think, for instance, that we have seen, are seeing, various ways of dealing with vulnerability and grief, so that, for instance, William Safire citing Milton writes we must "banish melancholy,"[5] as if the repudiation of melancholy ever did anything other than fortify its affective structure under another name, since melancholy is already the repudiation of mourning; so that, for instance, President Bush announced on September 21 that we have finished grieving and that *now* it is time for resolute action to take the place of grief.[6] When grieving is something to be feared, our fears can give rise to the impulse to resolve it quickly, to banish it in the name of an action invested with the power to restore the loss or return the world to a

former order, or to reinvigorate a fantasy that the world formerly
was orderly.

Is there something to be gained from grieving, from tarrying with
grief, from remaining exposed to its unbearability and not endeav-
oring to seek a resolution for grief through violence? Is there
something to be gained in the political domain by maintaining grief
as part of the framework within which we think our international
ties? If we stay with the sense of loss, are we left feeling only passive
and powerless, as some might fear? Or are we, rather, returned to a
sense of human vulnerability, to our collective responsibility for the
physical lives of one another? Could the experience of a dislocation
of First World safety not condition the insight into the radically
inequitable ways that corporeal vulnerability is distributed globally?
To foreclose that vulnerability, to banish it, to make ourselves secure
at the expense of every other human consideration is to eradicate one
of the most important resources from which we must take our
bearings and find our way.

To grieve, and to make grief itself into a resource for politics, is
not to be resigned to inaction, but it may be understood as the slow
process by which we develop a point of identification with suffering
itself. The disorientation of grief—"Who have I become?" or, indeed,
"What is left of me?" "What is it in the Other that I have lost?"—
posits the "I" in the mode of unknowingness.

But this can be a point of departure for a new understanding if the
narcissistic preoccupation of melancholia can be moved into a
consideration of the vulnerability of others. Then we might critically
evaluate and oppose the conditions under which certain human lives
are more vulnerable than others, and thus certain human lives are more
grievable than others. From where might a principle emerge by which
we vow to protect others from the kinds of violence we have suffered,
if not from an apprehension of a common human vulnerability? I do

not mean to deny that vulnerability is differentiated, that it is allocated differentially across the globe. I do not even mean to presume upon a common notion of the human, although to speak in its "name" is already (and perhaps only) to fathom its possibility.

I am referring to violence, vulnerability, and mourning, but there is a more general conception of the human with which I am trying to work here, one in which we are, from the start, given over to the other, one in which we are, from the start, even prior to individuation itself and, by virtue of bodily requirements, given over to some set of primary others: this conception means that we are vulnerable to those we are too young to know and to judge and, hence, vulnerable to violence; but also vulnerable to another range of touch, a range that includes the eradication of our being at the one end, and the physical support for our lives at the other.

Although I am insisting on referring to a common human vulnerability, one that emerges with life itself, I also insist that we cannot recover the source of this vulnerability: it precedes the formation of "I." This is a condition, a condition of being laid bare from the start and with which we cannot argue. I mean, we can argue with it, but we are perhaps foolish, if not dangerous, when we do. I do not mean to suggest that the necessary support for a newborn is always there. Clearly, it is not, and for some this primary scene is a scene of abandonment or violence or starvation, that theirs are bodies given over to nothing, or to brutality, or to no sustenance.

We cannot understand vulnerability as a deprivation, however, unless we understand the need that is thwarted. Such infants still must be apprehended as given over, as given over to no one or to some insufficient support, or to an abandonment. It would be difficult, if not impossible, to understand how humans suffer from oppression without seeing how this primary condition is exploited and exploitable, thwarted and denied. The condition of primary vulnerability, of being given over to the touch of the other, even if there is no other there, and no support for our lives, signifies a primary helplessness and need, one to which any society must attend. Lives are supported and maintained differently, and there are radically different ways in which human physical vulnerability is distributed across the globe. Certain lives will be highly protected, and the abrogation of their claims to sanctity will be sufficient to mobilize the forces of war. Other lives will not find such fast and furious support and will not even qualify as "grievable."

A hierarchy of grief could no doubt be enumerated. We have seen it already, in the genre of the obituary, where lives are quickly tidied up and summarized, humanized, usually married, or on the way to be, heterosexual, happy, monogamous. But this is just a sign of another differential relation to life, since we seldom, if ever, hear the names of the thousands of Palestinians who have died by the Israeli military with United States support, or any number of Afghan people, children and adults. Do they have names and faces, personal histories, family, favorite hobbies, slogans by which they live? What defense against the apprehension of loss is at work in the blithe way in which we accept deaths caused by military means with a shrug or with self-righteousness or with clear vindictiveness? To what extent have Arab peoples, predominantly practitioners of Islam, fallen outside the "human" as it has been naturalized in its "Western" mold by the contemporary workings of humanism? What are the cultural contours of the human at work here? How do our cultural frames for thinking the human set limits on the kinds of losses we can avow as loss? After all, if someone is lost, and that person is not someone, then what and where is the loss, and how does mourning take place?

This last is surely a question that lesbian, gay, and bi-studies have asked in relation to violence against sexual minorities; that trans-gendered people have asked as they are singled out for harassment and sometimes murder; that intersexed people have asked, whose formative years are so often marked by unwanted violence against their bodies in the name of a normative notion of the human, a normative notion of what the body of a human must be. This question is no doubt, as well, the basis of a profound affinity between movements centering on gender and sexuality and efforts to counter the normative human morphologies and capacities that condemn or efface those who are physically challenged. It must also be part of the affinity with anti-racist struggles, given the racial differential that undergirds the culturally viable notions of the human, ones that we see acted out in dramatic and terrifying ways in the global arena at the present time.

I am referring not only to humans not regarded as humans, and thus to a restrictive conception of the human that is based upon their exclusion. It is not a matter of a simple entry of the excluded into an established ontology, but an insurrection at the level of ontology, a critical opening up of the questions, What is real? Whose lives are real? How might reality be remade? Those who are unreal have, in a sense, already suffered the violence of derealization. What, then, is the relation between violence and those lives considered as "unreal"? Does violence effect that unreality? Does violence take place on the condition of that unreality?

If violence is done against those who are unreal, then, from the perspective of violence, it fails to injure or negate those lives since those lives are already negated. But they have a strange way of remaining animated and so must be negated again (and again). They cannot be mourned because they are always already lost or, rather, never "were," and they must be killed, since they seem to live on, stubbornly, in this state of deadness. Violence renews itself in the face of the apparent inexhaustibility of its object. The derealization of the "Other" means that it is neither alive nor dead, but interminably spectral. The infinite paranoia that imagines the war against terrorism as a war without end will be one that justifies itself endlessly in relation to the spectral infinity of its enemy, regardless of whether or not there are established grounds to suspect the continuing operation of terror cells with violent aims.

How do we understand this derealization? It is one thing to argue that first, on the level of discourse, certain lives are not considered lives at all, they cannot be humanized, that they fit no dominant frame for the human, and that their dehumanization occurs first, at this level, and that this level then gives rise to a physical violence that in some sense delivers the message of dehumanization that is already at work in the culture. It is another thing to say that discourse itself effects violence through omission. If 200,000 Iraqi children were killed during the Gulf War and its aftermath,[7] do we have an image, a frame for any of those lives, singly or collectively? Is there a story we might find about those deaths in the media? Are there names attached to those children?

There are no obituaries for the war casualties that the United States inflicts, and there cannot be. If there were to be an obituary, there would have had to have been a life, a life worth noting, a life worth valuing and preserving, a life that qualifies for recognition. Although we might argue that it would be impractical to write obituaries for all those people, or for all people, I think we have to ask, again and again, how the obituary functions as the instrument by which grievability is publicly distributed. It is the means by which a life becomes, or fails to become, a publicly grievable life, an icon for national self-recognition, the means by which a life becomes note-worthy. As a result, we have to consider the obituary as an act of nation-building. The matter is not a simple one, for, if a life is not grievable, it is not quite a life; it does not qualify as a life and is not worth a note. It is already the unburied, if not the unburiable.

It is not simply, then, that there is a "discourse" of dehumanization that produces these effects, but rather that there is a limit to discourse that establishes the limits of human intelligibility. It is not just that a death is poorly marked, but that it is unmarkable. Such a death vanishes, not into explicit discourse, but in the ellipses by which public discourse proceeds. The queer lives that vanished on September 11 were not publicly welcomed into the idea of national identity built in the obituary pages, and their closest relations were only belatedly and selectively (the marital norm holding sway once again) made eligible for benefits. But this should come as no surprise, when we think about how few deaths from AIDS were publicly grievable losses, and how, for instance, the extensive deaths now taking place in Africa are also, in the media, for the most part unmarkable and ungrievable.

A Palestinian citizen of the United States recently submitted to the *San Francisco Chronicle* obituaries for two Palestinian families who had been killed by Israeli troops, only to be told that the obituaries could not be accepted without proof of death.[8] The staff of the *Chronicle* said that statements "in memoriam" could, however, be accepted, and so the obituaries were rewritten and resubmitted in the form of memorials. These memorials were then rejected, with the explanation that the newspaper did not wish to offend anyone. We have to wonder under what conditions public grieving constitutes an "offense" against the public itself, constituting an intolerable eruption within the terms of what is speakable in public? What might be "offensive" about the public avowal of sorrow and loss, such that memorials would function as offensive speech? Is it that we should not proclaim in public these deaths, for fear of offending those who ally themselves with the Israeli state or military? Is it that these deaths are not considered to be real deaths, and that these lives not grievable, because they are Palestinians, or because they are victims of war? What is the relation between the violence by which these ungrievable lives were lost and the prohibition on their public grievability? Are the violence and the prohibition both permutations of the same violence? Does the prohibition on discourse relate to the dehumanization of the deaths—and the lives?

Dehumanization's relation to discourse is complex. It would be too simple to claim that violence simply implements what is already happening in discourse, such that a discourse on dehumanization produces treatment, including torture and murder, structured by the discourse. Here the dehumanization emerges at the limits of discursive life, limits established through prohibition and foreclosure. There is less a dehumanizing discourse at work here than a refusal of discourse that produces dehumanization as a result. Violence against those who are already not quite living, that is, living in a state of suspension between life and death, leaves a mark that is no mark. There will be no public act of grieving (said Creon in *Antigone*). If there is a "discourse," it is a silent and melancholic one in which there have been no lives, and no losses; there has been no common bodily condition, no vulnerability that serves as the basis for an apprehension of our commonality; and there has been no sundering of that commonality. None of this takes place on the order of the event. None of this takes place. In the silence of the newspaper, there was no event, no loss, and this failure of recognition is mandated through an identification with those who identify with the perpetrators of that violence.

This is made all the more apparent in United States journalism, in which, with some notable exceptions, one might have expected a public exposure and investigation of the bombing of civilian targets, the loss of lives in Afghanistan, the decimation of communities, infrastructures, religious centers. To the extent that journalists have accepted the charge to be part of the war effort itself, reporting itself has become a speech act in the service of the military operations. Indeed, after the brutal and terrible murder of the *Wall Street Journal*'s Daniel Pearl, several journalists started to write about themselves as working on the "front lines" of the war. Indeed, Daniel Pearl, "Danny" Pearl, is so familiar to me: he could be my brother or my cousin; he is so easily humanized; he fits the frame, his name has my father's name in it. His last name contains my Yiddish name.

But those lives in Afghanistan, or other United States targets, who were also snuffed out brutally and without recourse to any protection, will they ever be as human as Daniel Pearl? Will the names of the Palestinians stated in that memorial submitted to the *San Francisco Chronicle* ever be brought into public view? (Will we feel compelled to learn how to say these names and to remember them?) I do not say this to espouse a cynicism. I am in favor of the public obituary but mindful of who has access to it, and which deaths can be fairly mourned there. We should surely continue to grieve for Daniel Pearl, even though he is so much more easily humanized for most United States citizens than the nameless Afghans obliterated by United States and European violence. But we have to consider how the norm governing who will be a grievable human is circumscribed and produced in these acts of permissible and celebrated public grieving, how they sometimes operate in tandem with a prohibition on the public grieving of others' lives, and how this differential allocation of grief serves the derealizing aims of military violence. What follows as well from prohibitions on avowing grief in public is an effective mandate in favor of a generalized melancholia (and a derealization of loss) when it comes to considering *as dead* those the United States or its allies have killed.

Finally, it seems important to consider that the prohibition on certain forms of public grieving itself constitutes the public sphere on the basis of such a prohibition. The public will be created on the condition that certain images do not appear in the media, certain names of the dead are not utterable, certain losses are not avowed as losses, and violence is derealized and diffused. Such prohibitions not only shore up a nationalism based on its military aims and practices, but they also suppress any internal dissent that would expose the concrete, human effects of its violence.

Similarly, the extensive reporting of the final moments of the lost lives in the World Trade Center are compelling and important stories. They fascinate, and they produce an intense identification by arousing feelings of fear and sorrow. One cannot help but wonder, however, what humanizing effect these narratives have. By this I do not mean simply that they humanize the lives that were lost along with those that narrowly escaped, but that they stage the scene and provide the narrative means by which "the human" in its grievability is established. We cannot find in the public media, apart from some reports posted on the internet and circulated mainly through email contacts, the narratives of Arab lives killed elsewhere by brutal means. In this sense, we have to ask about the conditions under which a grievable life is established and maintained, and through what logic of exclusion, what practice of effacement and denominalization.

Mourning Daniel Pearl presents no problem for me or for my family of origin. His is a familiar name, a familiar face, a story about education that I understand and share; his wife's education makes her language familiar, even moving, to me, a proximity of what is similar.[9] In relation to him, I am not disturbed by the proximity of the unfamiliar, the proximity of difference that makes me work to forge new ties of identification and to reimagine what it is to belong to a human community in which common epistemological and cultural grounds cannot always be assumed. His story takes me home and tempts me to stay there. But at what cost do I establish the familiar as the criterion by which a human life is grievable?

Most Americans have probably experienced something like the loss of their First Worldism as a result of the events of September 11 and its aftermath. What kind of loss is this? It is the loss of the prerogative, only and always, to be the one who transgresses the sovereign boundaries of other states, but never to be in the position of having one's own boundaries transgressed. The United States was supposed to be the place that could not be attacked, where life was safe from violence initiated from abroad, where the only violence we knew was the kind that we inflicted on ourselves. The violence that we inflict on others is only—and always—selectively brought into public view. We now see that the national border was more permeable than we thought. Our general response is anxiety, rage; a radical desire for security, a shoring-up of the borders against what is perceived as alien; a heightened surveillance of Arab peoples and anyone who looks vaguely Arab in the dominant racial imaginary, anyone who looks like someone you once knew who was of Arab descent, or who you thought was—often citizens, it turns out, often Sikhs, often Hindus, even sometimes Israelis, especially Sephardim, often Arab-Americans, recent arrivals or those who have been in the US for decades.

Various terror alerts that go out over the media authorize and heighten racial hysteria in which fear is directed anywhere and nowhere, in which individuals are asked to be on guard but not told what to be on guard against; so everyone is free to imagine and identify the source of terror.

The result is that an amorphous racism abounds, rationalized by the claim of "self-defense." A generalized panic works in tandem with the shoring-up of the sovereign state and the suspension of civil liberties. Indeed, when the alert goes out, every member of the population is asked to become a "foot soldier" in Bush's army. The loss of First World presumption is the loss of a certain horizon of experience, a certain sense of the world itself as a national entitlement.

I condemn on several ethical bases the violence done against the
United States and do not see it as "just punishment" for prior sins.
At the same time, I consider our recent trauma to be an opportunity
for a reconsideration of United States hubris and the importance of
establishing more radically egalitarian international ties. Doing this
involves a certain "loss" for the country as a whole: the notion of the
world itself as a sovereign entitlement of the United States must be
given up, lost, and mourned, as narcissistic and grandiose fantasies
must be lost and mourned. From the subsequent experience of
loss and fragility, however, the possibility of making different kinds
of ties emerges. Such mourning might (or could) effect a transformation in our sense of international ties that would crucially
rearticulate the possibility of democratic political culture here and
elsewhere.

Unfortunately, the opposite reaction seems to be the case. The US
asserts its own sovereignty precisely at a moment in which the
sovereignty of the nation is bespeaking its own weakness, if not its
growing status as an anachronism. It requires international support,
but it insists on leading the way. It breaks its international contracts,
and then asks whether other countries are with America or against it.
It expresses its willingness to act consistently with the Geneva
Convention, but it refuses to be bound to that accord, as is stipulated
by its signatory status. On the contrary, the US decides whether it
will act consistently with the doctrine, which parts of the doctrine
apply, and will interpret that doctrine unilaterally. Indeed, in the very
moment in which it claims to act consistently with the doctrine, as it
does when it justifies its treatment of the Guantanamo Bay prisoners
as "humane," it decides unilaterally what will count as humane, and
openly defies the stipulated definition of humane treatment that the
Geneva Convention states in print. It bombs unilaterally, it says that
it is time for Saddam Hussein to be removed, it decides when and

where to install democracy, for whom, by means dramatically anti-democratic, and without compunction.

Nations are not the same as individual psyches, but both can be described as "subjects," albeit of different orders. When the United States acts, it establishes a conception of what it means to act as an American, establishes a norm by which that subject might be known. In recent months, a subject has been instated at the national level, a sovereign and extra-legal subject, a violent and self-centered subject; its actions constitute the building of a subject that seeks to restore and maintain its mastery through the systematic destruction of its multilateral relations, its ties to the international community. It shores itself up, seeks to reconstitute its imagined wholeness, but only at the price of denying its own vulnerability, its dependency, its exposure, where it exploits those very features in others, thereby making those features "other to" itself.

That this foreclosure of alterity takes place in the name of "feminism" is surely something to worry about. The sudden feminist conversion on the part of the Bush administration, which retroactively transformed the liberation of women into a rationale for its military actions against Afghanistan, is a sign of the extent to which feminism, as a trope, is deployed in the service of restoring the presumption of First World impermeability. Once again we see the spectacle of "white men, seeking to save brown women from brown men," as Gayatri Chakravorty Spivak once described the culturally imperialist exploitation of feminism.[10] Feminism itself becomes, under these circumstances, unequivocally identified with the imposition of values on cultural contexts willfully unknown. It would surely be a mistake to gauge the progress of feminism by its success as a colonial project. It seems more crucial than ever to disengage feminism from its First World presumption and to use the resources of feminist theory, and activism, to rethink the meaning of the tie, the bond, the alliance, the relation, as they are imagined and lived in the horizon of a counterimperialist egalitarianism.

Feminism surely could provide all kinds of responses to the following questions: How does a collective deal, finally, with its vulnerability to violence? At what price, and at whose expense, does it gain a purchase on "security," and in what ways has a chain of violence formed in which the aggression the United States has wrought returns to it in different forms? Can we think of the history of violence here without exonerating those who engage it against the United States in the present? Can we provide a knowledgeable explanation of events that is not confused with a moral exoneration of violence? What has happened to the value of critique as a democratic value? Under what conditions is critique itself censored, as if any reflexive criticism can only and always be construed as weakness and fallibility?

Negotiating a sudden and unprecedented vulnerability—what are the options? What are the long-term strategies? Women know this question well, have known it in nearly all times, and nothing about the triumph of colonial powers has made our exposure to this kind of violence any less clear. There is the possibility of appearing imper- meable, of repudiating vulnerability itself. Nothing about being socially constituted as women restrains us from simply becoming violent ourselves. And then there is the other age-old option, the possibility of wishing for death or becoming dead, as a vain effort to preempt or deflect the next blow. But perhaps there is some other way to live such that one becomes neither affectively dead nor mimetically violent, a way out of the circle of violence altogether. This possibi- lity has to do with demanding a world in which bodily vulnerability is protected without therefore being eradicated and with insisting on the line that must be walked between the two.

By insisting on a "common" corporeal vulnerability, I may seem to be positing a new basis for humanism. That might be true, but I am prone to consider this differently. A vulnerability must be perceived and recognized in order to come into play in an ethical encounter, and there is no guarantee that this will happen. Not only is there always the possibility that a vulnerability will not be recognized and that it will be constituted as the "unrecognizable," but when a vulnerability *is* recognized, that recognition has the power to change the meaning and structure of the vulnerability itself. In this sense, if vulnerability is one precondition for humanization, and humanization takes place differently through variable norms of recognition, then it follows that vulnerability is fundamentally dependent on existing norms of recognition if it is to be attributed to any human subject.

So when we say that every infant is surely vulnerable, that is clearly true; but it is true, in part, precisely because our utterance enacts the very recognition of vulnerability and so shows the importance of recognition itself for sustaining vulnerability. We perform the recognition by making the claim, and that is surely a very good ethical reason to make the claim. We make the claim, however, precisely because it is not taken for granted, precisely because it is not, in every instance, honored. Vulnerability takes on another meaning at the moment it is recognized, and recognition wields the power to reconstitute vulnerability. We cannot posit this vulnerability prior to recognition without performing the very thesis that we oppose (our positing is itself a form of recognition and so manifests the constitutive power of the discourse). This framework, by which norms of recognition are essential to the constitution of vulnerability as a precondition of the "human," is important precisely for this reason, namely, that we need and want those norms to be in place, that we struggle for their establishment, and that we value their continuing and expanded operation.

Consider that the struggle for recognition in the Hegelian sense requires that each partner in the exchange recognize not only that the other needs and deserves recognition, but also that each, in a different way, is compelled by the same need, the same requirement. This means that we are not separate identities in the struggle for recognition but are already involved in a reciprocal exchange, an exchange that dislocates us from our positions, our subject-positions, and allows us to see that community itself requires the recognition that we are all, in different ways, striving for recognition.

When we recognize another, or when we ask for recognition for ourselves, we are not asking for an Other to see us as we are, as we already are, as we have always been, as we were constituted prior to the encounter itself. Instead, in the asking, in the petition, we have already become something new, since we are constituted by virtue of the address, a need and desire for the Other that takes place in language in the broadest sense, one without which we could not be. To ask for recognition, or to offer it, is precisely not to ask for recognition for what one already is. It is to solicit a becoming, to instigate a transformation, to petition the future always in relation to the Other. It is also to stake one's own being, and one's own persistence in one's own being, in the struggle for recognition. This is perhaps a version of Hegel that I am offering, but it is also a departure, since I will not discover myself as the same as the "you" on which I depend in order to be.

I have moved in this essay perhaps too blithely among speculations on the body as the site of a common human vulnerability, even as I have insisted that this vulnerability is always articulated differently, that it cannot be properly thought of outside a differentiated field of power and, specifically, the differential operation of norms of recognition. At the same time, however, I would probably still insist that speculations on the formation of the subject are crucial to understanding the basis of non-violent responses to injury and, perhaps most important, to a theory of collective responsibility. I realize that it is not possible to set up easy analogies between the formation of the individual and the formation, say, of state-centered political cultures, and I caution against the use of individual psychopathology to diagnose or even simply to read the kinds of violent formations in which state- and non-state-centered forms of power engage. But when we are speaking about the "subject" we are not always speaking about an individual: we are speaking about a model for agency and intelligibility, one that is very often based on notions of sovereign power. At the most intimate levels, we are social; we are comported toward a "you"; we are outside ourselves, constituted in cultural norms that precede and exceed us, given over to a set of cultural norms and a field of power that condition us fundamentally.

The task is doubtless to think through this primary impressionability and vulnerability with a theory of power and recognition. To do this would no doubt be one way a politically informed psychoanalytic feminism could proceed. The "I" who cannot come into being without a "you" is also fundamentally dependent on a set of norms of recognition that originated neither with the "I" nor with the "you." What is prematurely, or belatedly, called the "I" is, at the outset, enthralled, even if it is to a violence, an abandonment, a mechanism; doubtless it seems better at that point to be enthralled with what is impoverished or abusive than not to be enthralled at all and so to lose the condition of one's being and becoming. The bind of radically inadequate care consists of this, namely, that attachment is crucial to survival and that, when attachment takes place, it does so in relation to persons and institutional conditions that may well be violent, impoverishing, and inadequate. If an infant fails to attach, it is threatened with death, but, under some conditions, even if it does attach, it is threatened with non-survival from another direction. So the question of primary support for primary vulnerability is an ethical one for the infant and for the child. But there are broader ethical consequences from this situation, ones that pertain not only to the adult world but to the sphere of politics and its implicit ethical dimension.

I find that my very formation implicates the other in me, that my own foreignness to myself is, paradoxically, the source of my ethical connection with others. I am not fully known to myself, because part of what I am is the enigmatic traces of others. In this sense, I cannot know myself perfectly or know my "difference" from others in an irreducible way. This unknowingness may seem, from a given perspective, a problem for ethics and politics. Don't I need to know myself in order to act responsibly in social relations? Surely, to a certain extent, yes. But is there an ethical valence to my unknowingness? I am wounded, and I find that the wound itself testifies to the fact that I am impressionable, given over to the Other in ways that I cannot fully predict or control. I cannot think the question of responsibility alone, in isolation from the Other; if I do, I have taken myself out of the relational bind that frames the problem of responsibility from the start.

If I understand myself on the model of the human, and if the kinds of public grieving that are available to me make clear the norms by which the "human" is constituted for me, then it would seem that I am as much constituted by those I do grieve for as by those whose deaths I disavow, whose nameless and faceless deaths form the melancholic background for my social world, if not my First Worldism. Antigone, risking death herself by burying her brother against the edict of Creon, exemplified the political risks in defying the ban against public grief during times of increased sovereign power and hegemonic national unity.[11] What are the cultural barriers against which we struggle when we try to find out about the losses that we are asked not to mourn, when we attempt to name, and so to bring under the rubric of the "human," those whom the United States and its allies have killed? Similarly, the cultural barriers that feminism must negotiate have to take place with reference to the operation of power and the persistence of vulnerability.

A feminist opposition to militarism emerges from many sources, many cultural venues, in any number of idioms; it does not have to—and, finally, cannot—speak in a single political idiom, and no grand settling of epistemological accounts has to be required. This seems to be the theoretical commitment, for instance, of the organization Women in Black.[12] A desideratum comes from Chandra Mohanty's important essay "Under Western Eyes," in which she maintains that notions of progress within feminism cannot be equated with assimilation to so-called Western notions of agency and political mobilization.[13] There she argues that the comparative framework in which First World feminists develop their critique of the conditions of oppression for Third World women on the basis of universal claims not only misreads the agency of Third World feminists, but also falsely produces a homogeneous conception of who they are and what they want. In her view, that framework also reproduces the First World as the site of authentic feminist agency and does so by producing a monolithic Third World against which to understand itself. Finally, she argues that the imposition of versions of agency onto Third World contexts, and focusing on the ostensible lack of agency signified by the veil or the burka, not only misunderstands the various cultural meanings that the burka might carry for women who wear it, but also denies the very idioms of agency that are relevant for such women.[14] Mohanty's critique is thorough and right—and it was written more than a decade ago. It seems to me now that the possibility of international coalition has to be rethought on the basis of this critique and others. Such a coalition would have to be modeled on new modes of cultural translation and would be different from appreciating this or that position or asking for recognition in ways that assume that we are all fixed and frozen in our various locations and "subject-positions."

We could have several engaged intellectual debates going on at the same time and find ourselves joined in the fight against violence, without having to agree on many epistemological issues. We could disagree on the status and character of modernity and yet find ourselves joined in asserting and defending the rights of indigenous women to health care, reproductive technology, decent wages, physical protection, cultural rights, freedom of assembly. If you saw me on such a protest line, would you wonder how a postmodernist was able to muster the necessary "agency" to get there today? I doubt it. You would assume that I had walked or taken the subway! By the same token, various routes lead us into politics, various stories bring us onto the street, various kinds of reasoning and belief. We do not need to ground ourselves in a single model of communication, a single model of reason, a single notion of the subject before we are able to act. Indeed, an international coalition of feminist activists and thinkers—a coalition that affirms the thinking of activists and the activism of thinkers and refuses to put them into distinctive categories that deny the actual complexity of the lives in question—will have to accept the array of sometimes incommensurable epistemological and political beliefs and modes and means of agency that bring us into activism.

There will be differences among women, for instance, on what the role of reason is in contemporary politics. Spivak insists that it is not *reason* that politicizes the tribal women of India suffering exploitation by capitalist firms, but a set of values and a sense of the sacred that come through religion.[15] And Adriana Cavarero claims that it is not because we are reasoning beings that we are connected to one another, but, rather, because we are *exposed* to one another, requiring a recognition that does not substitute the recognizer for the recognized.[16] Do we want to say that it is our status as "subjects" that binds us all together even though, for many of us, the "subject" is multiple or fractured? And does the insistence on the subject as a precondition of political agency not erase the more fundamental modes of dependency that do bind us and out of which emerge our thinking and affiliation, the basis of our vulnerability, affiliation, and collective resistance?

What allows us to encounter one another? What are the conditions of possibility for an international feminist coalition? My sense is that to answer these questions, we cannot look to the nature of "man," or the a priori conditions of language, or the timeless conditions of communication. We have to consider the demands of cultural translation that we assume to be part of an ethical responsibility (over and above the explicit prohibitions against thinking the Other under the sign of the "human") as we try to think the global dilemmas that women face. It is not possible to impose a language of politics developed within First World contexts on women who are facing the threat of imperialist economic exploitation and cultural obliteration. On the other hand, we would be wrong to think that the First World is *here* and the Third World is *there*, that a second world is *somewhere else*, that a subaltern subtends these divisions. These topographies have shifted, and what was once thought of as a border, that which delimits and bounds, is a highly populated site, if not the very definition of the nation, confounding identity in what may well become a very auspicious direction.

For if I am confounded by you, then you are already of me, and I am nowhere without you. I cannot muster the "we" except by finding the way in which I am tied to "you," by trying to translate but finding that my own language must break up and yield if I am to know you. You are what I gain through this disorientation and loss. This is how the human comes into being, again and again, as that which we have yet to know.

3

INDEFINITE DETENTION

I'm not a lawyer. I'm not into that end of the business.

Donald Rumsfeld, Secretary of Defense

On March 21, 2002, the Department of Defense, in conjunction with the Department of Justice, issued new guidelines for the military tribunals in which some of the prisoners detained domestically and in Guantanamo Bay would be tried by the US. What has been striking about these detentions from the start, and continues to be alarming, is that the right to legal counsel and, indeed, the right to a trial has not been granted to most of these detainees. The new military tribunals are, in fact, not courts of law to which the detainees from the war against Afghanistan are entitled. Some will be tried, and others will not, and at the time of this writing, plans have just been announced to try 6 of the 650 prisoners who have remained in captivity there for more than a year. The rights to counsel, means of appeal, and repatriation stipulated by the Geneva Convention have not been granted to any of the detainees in Guantanamo, and although the US has announced its recognition of the Taliban as "covered" by the Geneva Accord, it has made clear that even the Taliban do not have prisoner of war status; as, indeed, no prisoner in Guantanamo has.

In the name of a security alert and national emergency, the law is effectively suspended in both its national and international forms. And with the suspension of law comes a new exercise of state sovereignty, one that not only takes place outside the law, but through an elaboration of administrative bureaucracies in which officials now not only decide who will be tried, and who will be detained, but also have ultimate say over whether someone may be detained indefinitely or not. With the publication of the new regulations, the US government holds that a number of detainees at Guantanamo will not be given trials at all, but detained indefinitely.[1] What sort of legal innovation is the notion of indefinite detention? And what does it say about the contemporary formation and extension of state power? Indefinite detention not only carries implications for when and where law will be suspended but for determining the limit and scope of legal jurisdiction itself. Both of these, in turn, carry implications for the extension and self-justificatory procedures of state sovereignty.

Foucault wrote in 1978 that governmentality, understood as the way in which political power manages and regulates populations and goods, has become the main way state power is vitalized. He does not say, interestingly, that the state is legitimated by governmentality, only that it is "vitalized," suggesting that the state, without governmentality, would fall into a condition of decay. Foucault suggests that the state used to be vitalized by sovereign power, where sovereignty is understood, traditionally, as providing legitimacy for the rule of law and offering a guarantor for the representational claims of state power. But as sovereignty in that traditional sense has lost its credibility and function, governmentality has emerged as a form of power not only distinct from sovereignty, but characteristically late modern.[2] Governmentality is broadly understood as a mode of power concerned with the maintenance and control of bodies and persons, the production and regulation of persons and populations, and the circulation of goods insofar as they maintain and restrict the life of the population. Governmentality operates through policies and departments, through managerial and bureaucratic institutions, through the law, when the law is understood as "a set of tactics," and through forms of state power, although not exclusively. Governmentality thus operates through state and non-state institutions and discourses that are legitimated neither by direct elections nor through established authority. Marked by a diffuse set of strategies and tactics, governmentality gains its meaning and purpose from no single source, no unified sovereign subject. Rather, the tactics characteristic of governmentality operate diffusely, to dispose and order populations, and to produce and reproduce subjects, their practices and beliefs, in relation to specific policy aims. Foucault maintained, boldly, that "the problems of governmentality and the techniques of government have become the only political issues, the only real space for political struggle and contestation" (103). For Foucault, it is precisely "governmentalization that has permitted the state to survive" (103). The only real political issues are those that are vital for us, and what vitalizes those issues within modernity, according to Foucault, is governmentalization.

Although Foucault may well be right about governmentality having assumed this status, it is important to consider that the emergence of governmentality does not always coincide with the devitalization of sovereignty.[3] Rather, the emergence of governmentality may depend upon the *de*vitalization of sovereignty in its traditional sense: sovereignty as providing a legitimating function for the state; sovereignty as a unified locus for state power. Sovereignty in this sense no longer operates to support or vitalize the state, but this does not foreclose the possibility that it might emerge as a reanimated anachronism within the political field unmoored from its traditional anchors. Indeed, whereas sovereignty has conventionally been linked with legitimacy for the state and the rule of law, providing a unified source and symbol of political power, it no longer functions that way. Its loss is not without consequence, and its resurgence within the field of governmentality marks the power of the anachronism to animate the contemporary field. To consider that sovereignty emerges within the field of governmentality, we have to call into question, as Foucault surely also did, the notion of history as a continuum. The task of the critic, as Walter Benjamin maintained, is thus to "blast a specific era out of the homogeneous course of history" and to "grasp ... the constellation which his own era has formed with a definite earlier one."[4]

Even as Foucault offered an account of governmentality that emerged as a consequence of the devitalization of sovereignty, he called into question that chronology, insisting that the two forms of power could exist simultaneously. I would like to suggest that the current configuration of state power, in relation both to the management of populations (the hallmark of governmentality) and the exercise of sovereignty in the acts that suspend and limit the jurisdiction of law itself, are reconfigured in terms of the new war prison. Although Foucault makes what he calls an analytic distinction between sovereign power and governmentality, suggesting at various moments that governmentality is a later form of power, he also holds open the possibility that these two forms of power can and do coexist in various ways, especially in relation to that form of power he called "discipline." What was not possible from his vantage point was to predict what form this coexistence would take in the present circumstances, that is, that sovereignty, under emergency conditions in which the rule of law is suspended, would reemerge in the context of governmentality with the vengeance of an anachronism that refuses to die. This resurgent sovereignty makes itself known primarily in the instance of the exercise of prerogative power. But what is strange, if not fully disturbing, is how the prerogative is reserved either for the executive branch of government or to managerial officials with no clear claim to legitimacy.

In the moment that the executive branch assumes the power of the judiciary, and invests the person of the President with unilateral and final power to decide when, where, and whether a military trial takes place, it is as if we have returned to a historical time in which sovereignty was indivisible, before the separation of powers has instated itself as a precondition of political modernity. Or better formulated: *the historical time that we thought was past turns out to structure the contemporary field with a persistence that gives the lie to history as chronology*. Yet the fact that managerial officials decide who will be detained indefinitely, and who will be reviewed for the possibility of a trial with questionable legitimacy, suggests that a parallel exercise of illegitimate decision is exercised within the field of governmentality.

Governmentality is characterized by Foucault as sometimes deploying law as a tactic, and we can see the instrumental uses to which law is put in the present situation. Not only is law treated as a tactic, but it is also suspended in order to heighten the discretionary power of those who are asked to rely on their own judgment to decide fundamental matters of justice, life, and death. Whereas the suspension of law can clearly be read as a tactic of governmentality, it has to be seen in this context as also making room for the resurgence of sovereignty, and in this way both operations work together. The present insistence by the state that law can and ought to be suspended gives us insight into a broader phenomenon, namely, that sovereignty is reintroduced in the very acts by which state suspends law, or contorts law to its own uses. In this way, the state extends its own domain, its own necessity, and the means by which its self-justification occurs. I hope to show how procedures of governmentality, which are irreducible to law, are invoked to extend and fortify forms of sovereignty that are equally irreducible to law. Neither is necessarily grounded in law, and neither deploys legal tactics exclusively in the field of their respective operations. The suspension of the rule of law allows for the convergence of governmentality and sovereignty; sovereignty is exercised in the act of suspension, but also in the self-allocation of legal prerogative; governmentality denotes an operation of administration power that is extra-legal, even as it can and does return to law as a field of tactical operations. The state is neither identified with the acts of sovereignty nor with the field of governmentality, and yet both act in the name of the state. Law itself is either suspended, or regarded as an instrument that the state may use in the service of constraining and monitoring a given population; the state is not subject to the rule of law, but law can be suspended or deployed tactically and partially to suit the requirements of a state that seeks more and more to allocate sovereign power to its executive and administrative powers. The law is suspended in the name of the "sovereignty" of the nation, where "sovereignty" denotes the task of any state to preserve and protect its own territoriality. By this act of suspending the law, the state is further disarticulated into a set of administrative powers that are, to some extent, outside the apparatus of the state itself; and the forms of sovereignty resurrected in its midst mark the persistence of forms of sovereign political power for the executive that precede the emergence of the state in its modern form.

It is, of course, tempting to say that something called the "state," imagined as a powerful unity, makes use of the field of governmentality to reintroduce and reinstate its own forms of sovereignty. This description doubtless misdescribes the situation, however, since governmentality designates a field of political power in which tactics and aims have become diffuse, and in which political power fails to take on a unitary and causal form. But my point is that precisely because our historical situation is marked by governmentality, and this implies, to a certain degree, a loss of sovereignty, that loss is compensated through the resurgence of sovereignty within the field of governmentality. Petty sovereigns abound, reigning in the midst of bureaucratic army institutions mobilized by aims and tactics of power they do not inaugurate or fully control. And yet such figures are delegated with the power to render unilateral decisions, accountable to no law and without any legitimate authority. The resurrected sovereignty is thus not the sovereignty of unified power under the conditions of legitimacy, the form of power that guarantees the representative status of political institutions. It is, rather, a lawless and prerogatory power, a "rogue" power *par excellence*.

Let me turn first to the contemporary acts of state before returning to Foucault, not to "apply" him (as if he were a technology), but to rethink the relation between sovereignty and law that he introduces. To know what produces the extension of sovereignty in the field of governmentality, first we must discern the means by which the state suspends law and the kinds of justification they offer for that suspension.

With the publication of the new regulations, the US government holds that a number of detainees at Guantanamo will not be given trials at all, but will rather be detained indefinitely. It is crucial to ask under what conditions some human lives cease to become eligible for basic, if not universal, human rights. How does the US government construe these conditions? And to what extent is there a racial and ethnic frame through which these imprisoned lives are viewed and judged such that they are deemed less than human, or as having departed from the recognizable human community? Moreover, in maintaining that some prisoners will be detained indefinitely, the state allocates to itself a power, an indefinitely prolonged power, to exercise judgments regarding who is dangerous and, therefore, without entitlement to basic legal rights. In detaining some prisoners indefinitely, the state appropriates for itself a sovereign power that is defined over and against existing legal frameworks, civil, military, and international. The military tribunals may well acquit someone of a crime, but not only is that acquittal subject to mandatory executive review, but the Department of Defense has also made clear that acquittal will not necessarily end detention. Moreover, according to the new tribunal regulations, those tried in such a venue will have no rights of appeal to US civil courts (and US courts, responding to appeals, have so far maintained that they have no jurisdiction over Guantanamo, which falls outside US territory). Here we can see that the law itself is either suspended or regarded as an instrument that the state may use in the service of constraining and monitoring a given population. Under this mantle of sovereignty, the state proceeds to extend its own power to imprison indefinitely a group of people without trial. In the very act by which state sovereignty suspends law, or contorts law to its own uses, it extends its own domain, its own necessity, and develops the means by which the justification of its own power takes place. Of course, this is not the "state" in toto, but an executive branch working in tandem with an enhanced administrative wing of the military.

The state in this sense, then, augments its own power in at least two ways. In the context of the military tribunals, the trials yield no independent conclusions that cannot be reversed by the executive branch. The trials' function is thus mainly advisory. The executive branch in tandem with its military administration not only decides whether or not a detainee will stand trial, but appoints the tribunal, reviews the process, and maintains final say over matters of guilt, innocence, and punishment, including the death penalty. On May 24, 2003, Geoffrey Miller, commanding officer at Camp Delta, the new base on Guantanamo, explained in an interview that death chambers were in the process of being built there in anticipation of the death penalty being meted out.[5] Because detainees are not entitled to these trials, but offered them at the will of the executive power, there is no semblance of separation of powers in these circumstances. Those who are detained indefinitely will have their cases reviewed by officials—not by courts—on a periodic basis. The decision to detain someone indefinitely is not made by executive review, but by a set of administrators who are given broad policy guidelines within which to act. Neither the decision to detain nor the decision to activate the military tribunal is grounded in law. They are determined by discretionary judgments that function within a manufactured law or that manufacture law as they are performed. In this sense, both of these judgments are already outside the sphere of law, since the determination of when and where, for instance, a trial might be waived and detention deemed indefinite does not take place within a legal process, strictly speaking; it is not a decision made by a judge for which evidence must be submitted in the form of a case that must conform to certain established criteria or to certain protocols of evidence and argument. The decision to detain, to continue to detain someone indefinitely is a unilateral judgment made by government officials who simply deem that a given individual or, indeed, a group poses a danger to the state. This act of "deeming" takes place in the context of a declared state of emergency in which the state exercises prerogatory power that involves the suspension of law, including due process for these individuals. The act is warranted by the one who acts, and the "deeming" of someone as dangerous is sufficient to make that person dangerous and to justify his indefinite detention. The one who makes this decision assumes a lawless and yet fully effective form of power with the consequence not only of depriving an incarcerated human being of the possibility of a trial, in clear defiance of international law, but of investing the governmental bureaucrat with an extraordinary power over life and death. Those who decide on whether someone will be detained, and continue to be detained, are government officials, not elected ones, and not members of the judiciary. They are, rather, part of the apparatus of governmentality; their decision, the power they wield to "deem" someone dangerous and constitute them effectively as such, is a sovereign power, a ghostly and forceful resurgence of sovereignty in the midst of governmentality.

Wendy Brown points out that the distinction between governmentality and sovereignty is, for Foucault, overdrawn for tactical reasons in order to show the operation of state power outside the rule of law:

> Government in this broad sense, then, includes but is not reducible to questions of rule, legitimacy, or state institutions—it is about the corralling, ordering, directing, managing, and harnessing of human energy, need, capacity, and desire, and it is conducted across a number of institutional and discursive registers. Government in this sense stands in sharp contrast to the state: while Foucault acknowledges that the state may be "no more than a composite reality and a mythicized abstraction," as a signifier, it is a containing and negating

power, one that does not begin to capture the ways in which subjects and citizens are produced, positioned, classified, organized, and above all, mobilized by an array of governing sites and capacities. Government as Foucault uses it also stands in contrast to rule, or more precisely, with the end of monarchy and the dissolution of the homology between family and polity, rule ceases to be the dominant or even most important modality of governance. But Foucault is not arguing that governmentality—calculations and tactics that have the population as a target, that involve both specific governmental apparatuses and complexes of knowledges outside these apparatuses, and that convert the state itself into a set of administrative functions rather than ruling or justice-oriented ones—chronologically supersedes sovereignty and rule.[6]

Giorgio Agamben refuses as well the chronological argument that would situate sovereignty prior to governmentality. For Brown, both "governmentality" and "sovereignty" characterize modes of conceptualizing power rather than historically concrete phenomena that might be said to succeed each other in time. Agamben, in a different vein, argues that contemporary forms of sovereignty exist in *a structurally inverse relation* to the rule of law, emerging precisely at that moment when the rule of law is suspended and withdrawn. Sovereignty names the power that withdraws and suspends the law.[7] In a sense, legal protections are withdrawn, and law itself withdraws from the usual domain of its jurisdiction; this domain thus becomes opened to both governmentality (understood as an extra-legal field of policy, discourse, that may make law into a tactic) and sovereignty (understood as an extra-legal authority that may well institute and enforce law of its own making). Agamben notes that sovereignty asserts itself in deciding what will and will not constitute a state of exception, the occasion in which the rule of law is suspended. In granting the exceptional status to a given case, sovereign power comes into being in an inverse relation to the suspension of law. As law is suspended, sovereignty is exercised; moreover, sovereignty comes to exist to the extent that a domain—understood as "the exception"—immune from law is established: "what is excluded in the exception maintains itself in relation to the rule in the form of the rule's suspension. The rule applies to the exception in no longer applying, in withdrawing from it" (18).

Citing Carl Schmitt, Agamben describes sovereign control over the sphere of legality through establishing what will qualify as the exception to the legal rule: "the sovereign decision 'proves itself not to need law to create law.' What is at issue in the sovereign exception is not so much the control or neutralization of an excess as the creation and definition of the very space in which the juridico-political order can have validity" (19). The act by which the state annuls its own law has to be understood as an operation of sovereign power or, rather, the operation by which a lawless sovereign power comes into being or, indeed, reemerges in new form. State power is not fully exhausted by its legal exercises: it maintains, among other things, a relation to law, and it differentiates itself from law by virtue of the relation it takes. For Agamben, the state reveals its extra-legal status when it designates a state of exception to the rule of law and thereby withdraws the law selectively from its application. The result is a production of a paralegal universe that goes by the name of law.

My own view is that a contemporary version of sovereignty, animated by an aggressive nostalgia that seeks to do away with the separation of powers, is produced at the moment of this withdrawal, and that we have to consider the act of suspending the law as a performative one which brings a contemporary configuration of sovereignty into being or, more precisely, reanimates a spectral sovereignty within the field of governmentality. The state *produces*, through the act of withdrawal, a law that is no law, a court that is no court, a process that is no process. The state of emergency returns the operation of power from a set of laws (juridical) to a set of rules (governmental), and the rules reinstate sovereign power: rules that are not binding by virtue of established law or modes of legitimation, but fully discretionary, even arbitrary, wielded by officials who interpret them unilaterally and decide the condition and form of their invocation. Governmentality is the condition of this new exercise of sovereignty in the sense that it first establishes law as a "tactic," something of instrumental value, and not "binding" by virtue of its status as law. In a sense, the self-annulment of law under the condition of a state of emergency revitalizes the anachronistic "sovereign" as the newly invigorated subjects of managerial power. Of course, they are not true sovereigns: their power is delegated, and they do not fully control the aims that animate their actions. Power precedes them, and constitutes them as "sovereigns," a fact that already gives the lie to sovereignty. They are not fully self-grounding; they do not offer either representative or legitimating functions to the policy. Nevertheless, they are constituted, within the constraints of governmentality, as those who will and do decide on who will be detained, and who will not, who may see life outside the prison again and who may not, and this constitutes an enormously consequential delegation and seizure of power. They are acted on, but they also act, and their actions are not subject to review by any higher judicial authority. The decision of when and where to convene a military tribunal is ultimately executive, but here again, the executive decides unilaterally, so that in each case the retraction of law reproduces sovereign power. In the former case, sovereign power emerges as the power of the managerial "official"—and a Kafkan nightmare (or Sadean drama) is realized. In the latter case, sovereignty returns to the executive, and the separation of powers is eclipsed.

We might, and should, object that rights are being suspended indefinitely, and that it is wrong for individuals to live under such conditions. Whereas it makes sense that the US government would take immediate steps to detain those against whom there is evidence that they intend to wage violence against the US, it does not follow that suspects such as these should be presumed guilty or that due process ought to be denied to them. This is the argument from the point of view of human rights. From the point of view of a critique of power, however, we also have to object, politically, to the indefinite extension of lawless power that such detentions portend. If detention may be indefinite, and such detentions are presumably justified on the basis of a state of emergency, then the US government can protract an indefinite state of emergency. It would seem that the state, in its executive function, now extends conditions of national emergency so that the state will now have recourse to extra-legal detention and the suspension of established law, both domestic and international, for the foreseeable future. Indefinite detention thus extends lawless power indefinitely. Indeed, the indefinite detention of the untried prisoner—or the prisoner tried by military tribunal and detained regardless of the outcome of the trial—is a practice that presupposes the indefinite extension of the war on terrorism. And if this war becomes a permanent part of the state apparatus, a condition which justifies and extends the use of military tribunals, then the executive branch has effectively set up its own judiciary function, one that overrides the separation of power, the writ of habeas corpus (guaranteed, it seems, by Guantanamo Bay's geographical location outside the borders of the United States, on Cuban land, but not under Cuban rule), and the entitlement to due process. It is not just that constitutional protections are indefinitely suspended, but that the state (in its augmented executive function) arrogates to itself the right to suspend the Constitution or to manipulate the geography of detentions and trials so that constitutional and international rights are effectively suspended. The state arrogates to its functionaries the right to suspend rights, which means that if detention is indefinite there is no foreseeable end to this practice of the executive branch (or the Department of Defense) deciding, unilaterally, when and where to suspend constitutionally protected rights, that is, to suspend the Constitution and the rule of law, so producing a form of sovereign power in these acts of suspension.

These prisoners at Camp Delta (and formerly Camp X-Ray), detained indefinitely, are not even called "prisoners" by the Department of Defense or by representatives of the current US administration. To call them by that name would suggest that internationally recognized rights pertaining to the treatment of prisoners of war ought to come into play. They are, rather, "detainees," those who are held in waiting, those for whom waiting may well be without end. To the extent that the state arranges for this pre-legal state as an "indefinite" one, it maintains that there will be those held by the government for whom the law does not apply, not only in the present, but for the indefinite future. In other words, there will be those for whom the protection of law is indefinitely postponed. The state, in the name of its right to protect itself and, hence, and through the rhetoric of sovereignty, extends its power in excess of the law and defies international accords; for if the detention is indefinite, then the lawless exercise of state sovereignty becomes indefinite as well. In this sense, indefinite detention provides the condition for the indefinite exercise of extra-legal state power. Although the justification for not providing trials—and the attendant rights of due process, legal counsel, rights of appeal—is that we are in a state of national emergency, a state understood as out of the ordinary, it seems to follow that the state of emergency is not limited in time and space, that it, too, enters onto an indefinite future. Indeed, state power restructures temporality itself, since the problem of terrorism is no longer a historically or geographically limited problem: it is limitless and without end, and this means that the state of emergency is potentially limitless and without end, and that the prospect of an exercise of state power in its lawlessness structures the future indefinitely. The future becomes a lawless future, not anarchical, but given over to the discretionary decisions of a set of designated sovereigns—a perfect paradox that shows how sovereigns emerge within governmentality—who are beholden to nothing and to no one except the performative power of their own decisions. They are instrumentalized, deployed by tactics of power they do not control, but this does not stop them from using power, and using it to reanimate a sovereignty that the governmentalized constellation of power appeared to have foreclosed. These are petty sovereigns, unknowing, to a degree, about what work they do, but performing their acts unilaterally and with enormous consequence. Their acts are clearly *conditioned*, but their acts are judgments that are nevertheless *unconditional* in the sense that they are final, not subject to review, and not subject to appeal.

It is worth pausing to make a few distinctions here: on the one hand, descriptively, the actions performed by the President, the functionaries at Guantanamo or in the Department of State, or, indeed, by the foreign policy spokespeople for the current US government, are not sovereign in a traditional sense insofar as they are motivated by a diffuse set of practices and policy aims, deployed in the service of power, part of a wider field of governmentality. Yet in each case they appear as sovereign or, rather, bring a form of sovereignty into the domain of appearance, resurrecting the notion of a self-grounding and unconditioned basis for decision that has self-preservation as its primary aim. The sovereignty that appears in these instances covers over its own basis in governmentality, yet the form in which it appears is precisely within the agency of the functionary and, so, within the field of governmentality itself. These appearances of sovereignty—what I have been calling anachronistic resurgences—take contemporary form as they assume shape within the field of governmentality, and are fundamentally transformed by appearing within that field. Moreover, the fact that they are conditioned but appear as unconditioned in no way affects the relation that they sustain to the rule of law. It is not, literally speaking, that a sovereign power suspends the rule of law, but that the rule of law, in the act of being suspended, produces sovereignty *in its action and as its effect*. This inverse relation to law produces the "unaccountability" of this operation of sovereign power, as well as its illegitimacy.

The distinction between governmentality and sovereignty is thus an important distinction that helps us describe more accurately how power works, and through what means. The distinction between sovereignty and the rule of law can also be described in terms of the mechanism through which those terms incessantly separate from each other. But in the context of this analysis, it is also normative: the sovereignty produced through the suspension (or fabrication) of the rule of law, seeks to establish a rival form of political legitimacy, one with no structures of accountability built in. Although we are following the reanimation of sovereignty in the cases of indefinite detention and the military tribunals, we can see that the US government invoked its own sovereignty in its declarations concerning the justifiability of its military assault on Iraq. The US defied international accords with claims that its own self-preservation was at stake. Not to attack preemptively, Bush maintained, was "suicidal," and he went on to justify the abrogation of the sovereignty of Iraq (deemed illegitimate because not instated through general elections), by asserting the sanctity of its own extended sovereign boundaries (which the US extends beyond all geographical limits to include the widest gamut of its "interests").

"Indefinite detention" is an illegitimate exercise of power, but it is, significantly, part of a broader tactic to neutralize the rule of law in the name of security. "Indefinite detention" does not signify an exceptional circumstance, but, rather, the means by which the exceptional becomes established as a naturalized norm. It becomes the occasion and the means by which the extra-legal exercise of state power justifies itself indefinitely, installing itself as a potentially permanent feature of political life in the US.

These acts of state are themselves not grounded in law, but in another form of judgment; in this sense, they are already outside the sphere of law, since the determination of when and where, for instance, a trial might be waived and detention deemed indefinite does not take place within a legal process *per se*. These are not decisions, for instance, made by a judge, for which evidence must be submitted in the form of a case conforming to certain protocols of evidence and argument. Agamben has elaborated upon how certain subjects undergo a suspension of their ontological status as subjects when states of emergency are invoked.[8] He argues that a subject deprived of rights of citizenship enters a suspended zone, neither living in the sense that a political animal lives, in community and bound by law, nor dead and, therefore, outside the constituting condition of the rule of law. These socially conditioned states of suspended life and suspended death exemplify the distinction that Agamben offers between "bare life" and the life of the political being (*bios politikon*), where this second sense of "being" is established only in the context of political community. If bare life, life conceived as biological minimum, becomes a condition to which we are all reducible, then we might find a certain universality in this condition. Agamben writes, "We are all potentially exposed to this condition," that is, "bare life" underwrites the actual political arrangements in which we live, posing as a contingency into which any political arrangement might dissolve. Yet such general claims do not yet tell us how this power functions differentially, to target and manage certain populations, to derealize the humanity of subjects who might potentially belong to a community bound by commonly recognized laws; and they do not tell us how sovereignty, understood as state sovereignty in this instance, works by differentiating populations on the basis of ethnicity and race, how the systematic management and derealization of populations function to support and extend the claims of a sovereignty accountable to no law; how sovereignty extends its own power precisely through the tactical and permanent deferral of the law itself. In other words, the suspension of the life of a political animal, the suspension of standing before the law, is itself a tactical exercise, and must be understood in terms of the larger aims of power. To be detained indefinitely, for instance, is precisely to have no definitive prospect for a reentry into the political fabric of life, even as one's situation is highly, if not fatally, politicized.

The military tribunals were originally understood to apply not only to those arrested within the US, but to "high-ranking" officials within the Taliban or al-Qaeda military networks currently detained in Guantanamo Bay. The *Washington Post* reported that

> there may be little use for the tribunals because the great majority of the 300 prisoners [in March of 2002] being held at the US naval base at Guantanamo Bay, Cuba, are low-ranking foot soldiers. Administration officials have other plans for many of the relatively junior captives now at Guantanamo Bay: indefinite detention without trial. US officials would take this action with prisoners they fear could pose a danger of terrorism even if they have little evidence of past crimes.

"Could pose a danger of terrorism": this means that conjecture is the basis of detention, but also that conjecture is the basis of an indefinite detention without trial. One could simply respond to these events by saying that everyone detained deserves a trial, and I do believe that is the right thing to say, and I am saying that. But saying that would not be enough, since we have to look at what constitutes a trial in these new military tribunals. What kind of trial does everyone deserve? In these new tribunals, evidentiary standards are very lax. For instance, hearsay and second-hand reports will constitute relevant evidence, whereas in regular trials, either in the civil court system or the established military court system, they are dismissed out of hand. Whereas some international human rights courts do permit hearsay, they do so under conditions in which *non-refoulement* is honored, that is, rules under which prisoners may not be exported to countries where confessions can be extracted through torture. Indeed, if one understands that trials are usually the place where we can test whether hearsay is true or not, where second-hand reports have to be documented by persuasive evidence or dismissed, then the very meaning of the trial has been transformed by the notion of a procedure that explicitly admits unsubstantiated claims, and where the fairness and non-coercive character of the interrogatory means used to garner that information has no bearing on the admissibility of the information into trial.

If these trials make a mockery of evidence, if they are, effectively, ways of circumventing the usual legal demands for evidence, then these trials nullify the very meaning of the trial, and they nullify the trial most effectively by taking on the name of the "trial." If we consider as well that a trial is that to which every subject is entitled if and when an allegation of wrong-doing is made by a law enforcement agency, then these trials also cease to be trials in this sense. The Department of Defense maintains explicitly that these trials are

planned "only for relatively high-ranking al-Qaeda and Taliban
operatives against whom there is persuasive evidence of terrorism or
war crimes."[9] This is the language of the Department of Defense,
but let us consider it closely, since one can see the self-justifying and
self-augmenting function of sovereign power in the way that the law
is not only suspended, but deployed as a tactic, and as a way of
differentiating among more or less entitled subjects. If the trials are
saved for high-ranking officials against whom there is persuasive
evidence, then this formulation suggests that either the relatively
low-ranking detainees are those against whom there is no persuasive
evidence, or even if there is persuasive evidence against low-ranking
members, these members have no entitlement to hear the charge, to
prepare a case for themselves, or to obtain release or final judgment
through a tribunal procedure. Given that the notion of "persuasive
evidence" has been effectively rewritten to include conventionally
non-persuasive evidence, such as hearsay and second-hand reports,
and there is a chance that the US means that there is no evidence that
would be found to be persuasive against these members by a new
military tribunal, the US is effectively admitting that not even hearsay or second-hand reports would supply sufficient evidence to
convict these low-ranking members. Given as well that the Northern
Alliance is credited with turning over many of the al-Qaeda and
Taliban detainees to US authorities, it would be important to know
whether that organization had good grounds for identifying the
individuals detained before the US decides to detain them indefinitely. If there is no such evidence, one might well wonder why they
are being detained at all. And if there is evidence, but such
individuals are not given a trial, one might well wonder how the
worth of these lives is regarded such that they remain ineligible for
legal entitlements guaranteed by existing US law and international
human rights law.

Because there is no persuasive evidence, and because there is no evidence that would be persuasive even when we allow non-persuasive evidence to become the standard in a trial, it follows that where there is no non-persuasive evidence, indefinite detention is justified. By first incorporating non-persuasive evidence into the very meaning of persuasive evidence, the state frees itself to make use of an equivocation to augment its extra-legal prerogative. To be fair, there are international precedents for indefinite detention without trial. The US cites European human rights courts that allowed the British authorities to detain Irish Catholic and Protestant militants for long periods of time, if they were "deemed dangerous, but not necessarily convicted of a crime." They have to be "deemed dangerous," but the "deeming" is not, as discussed above, a judgment that needs to be supported by evidence, a judgment for which there are rules of evidence. They have to be deemed "dangerous," but the danger has to be understood quite clearly as a danger in the context of a national emergency. In those cases cited by the Bush administration, the detentions lasted indefinitely, as long as "British officials"—notably not courts—reviewed the cases from time to time. So these are administrative reviews, which means that these are reviews managed by officials who are not part of any judicial branch of government, but agents of governmentality, as it were, administrative appointees or bureaucrats who have absorbed the adjudicative prerogative from the judicial branch. Similarly, these military tribunals are ones in which the chain of custody is suspended, which means that evidence seized through illegal means will still be admissible at trials. The appeal process is automatic, but remains within the military tribunal process in which the final say in matters of guilt and punishment resides with the executive branch, and the office of the President. This means that, whatever the conclusions of these trials, they can be potentially reversed or revised by the executive branch through a decision that is accountable to no one and no rule, a procedure that effectively overrides the separation of powers doctrine, suspending once again the binding power of the constitution in favor of an unchecked enlargement of executive power.

In a separate argument, the government points out that there is another legal precedent for this type of detention without criminal charge. This happens all the time, they claim, in the practice of the involuntary hospitalization of mentally ill people who pose a danger to themselves and others. We have to hesitate at this analogy for the moment, I think, not only because, in a proto-Foucaultian vein, it explicitly models the prison on the mental institution, but also because it sets up an analogy between the suspected terrorist or the captured soldier and the mentally ill. When analogies are offered, they presuppose the separability of the terms that are compared. But any analogy also assumes a common ground for comparability, and in this case the analogy functions to a certain degree by functioning metonymically. The terrorists are *like* the mentally ill because their mind-set is unfathomable, because they are outside of reason, because they are outside of "civilization," if we understand that term to be the catchword of a self-defined Western perspective that considers itself bound to certain versions of rationality and the claims that arise from them. Involuntary hospitalization is *like* involuntary incarceration, only if we accept the incarcerative function of the mental institution, or only if we accept that certain suspected criminal activities are themselves signs of mental illness. Indeed, one has to wonder whether it is not simply selected acts undertaken by Islamic extremists that are considered outside the bounds of rationality as established by a civilizational discourse of the West, but rather any and all beliefs and practices pertaining to Islam that become, effectively, tokens of mental illness to the extent that they depart from the hegemonic norms of Western rationality.

If the US understands the involuntary incarceration of the mentally ill as a suitable precedent for indefinite detention, then it assumes that certain norms of mental functioning are at work in both instances. After all, an ostensibly mentally ill person is involuntarily incarcerated precisely because there is a problem with volition; the person is not considered able to judge and choose and act according to norms of acceptable mental functioning. Can we say that the detainees are also figured in precisely this way?[10] The Department of Defense published pictures of prisoners shackled and kneeling, with hands manacled, mouths covered by surgical masks, and eyes blinded by blackened goggles. They were reportedly given sedatives, forced to have their heads shaved, and the cells where they are held in Camp X-Ray were 8 feet by 8 feet and 7½ feet high, larger than the ones for which they are slated and which, Amnesty International reports in April of 2002, are appreciably smaller than international law allows. There was a question of whether the metal sheet called a "roof" offered any of the protective functions against wind and rain associated with that architectural function.

The photographs produced an international outcry because the degradation—and the publicizing of the degradation—contravened the Geneva Convention, as the International Red Cross pointed out, and because these individuals were rendered faceless and abject, likened to caged and restrained animals. Indeed, Secretary Rumsfeld's own language at press conferences seems to corroborate this view that the detainees are not like other humans who enter into war, and that they are, in this respect, not "punishable" by law, but deserving of immediate and sustained forcible incarceration. When Secretary Rumsfeld was asked why these prisoners were being forcibly restrained and held without trial, he explained that if they were not restrained, they would kill again. He implied that the restraint is the only thing that keeps them from killing, that they are beings whose

very propensity it is to kill: that is what they would do as a matter
of course. Are they pure killing machines? If they are pure killing
machines, then they are not humans with cognitive function entitled to
trials, to due process, to knowing and understanding a charge against
them. They are something less than human, and yet—somehow—
they assume a human form. They represent, as it were, an equivocation
of the human, which forms the basis for some of the skepticism about
the applicability of legal entitlements and protections.

The danger that these prisoners are said to pose is unlike dangers
that might be substantiated in a court of law and redressed through
punishment. In the news conference on March 21, 2002, Department
of Defense General Counsel Haynes answers a reporter's question in
a way that confirms that this equivocation is at work in their thinking.
An unnamed reporter in the news conference, concerned about the
military tribunal, asks: If someone is acquitted of a crime under this
tribunal, will they be set free? Haynes replied:

> If we had a trial right this minute, it is conceivable that somebody
> could be tried and acquitted of that charge, but might not
> automatically be released. The people we are detaining, for example,
> in Guantanamo Bay, Cuba, are enemy combatants that [sic] we
> captured on the battlefield seeking to harm US soldiers or allies, and
> they're dangerous people. At the moment, we're not about to
> release any of them unless we find that they don't meet those
> criteria. At some point in the future ...

The reporter then interrupted, saying: "But if you [can't] convict
them, if you can't find them guilty, you would still paint them with
that brush that we find you dangerous even though we can't convict
you, and continue to incarcerate them?" After some to and fro,
Haynes stepped up to the microphone, and explained that "the people

that we now hold at Guantanamo are held for a specific reason that is not tied specifically to any particular crime. They're not held— they're not being held on the basis that they are necessarily criminals." They will not be released unless the US finds that "they don't meet those criteria," but it is unclear what criteria are at work in Haynes's remark. If the new military tribunal sets the criteria, then there is no guarantee that a prisoner will be released in the event of exoneration. The prisoner exonerated by trial may still be "deemed dangerous," where that deeming is based in no established criteria. Establishing dangerousness is not the same as establishing guilt and, in Haynes's view, and in views subsequently repeated by admini-strative spokespersons, the executive branch's power to deem a detainee dangerous preempts any determination of guilt or innocence established by a military tribunal.

In the wake of this highly qualified approach to the new military tribunals (themselves regarded as illegitimate), we see that these are tribunals whose rules of evidence depart in radical ways from both the rules of civilian courts and the protocols of existing military courts, that they will be used to try only some detainees, that the office of the President will decide who qualifies for these secondary military tribunals, and that matters of guilt and innocence reside finally with the executive branch. If a military tribunal acquits a person, the person may still be deemed dangerous, which means that the determination by the tribunal can be preempted by an extra-legal determination of dangerousness. Given that the military tribunal is itself extra-legal, we seem to be witnessing the replication of a principle of sovereign state prerogative that knows no bounds. At every step of the way, the executive branch decides the form of the tribunal, appoints its members, determines the eligibility of those to be tried, and assumes power over the final judgment; it imposes the trial selectively; it dispenses with conventional evidentiary procedure.

And it justifies all this through recourse to a determination of "dangerousness" which it alone is in the position to decide. A certain level of dangerousness takes a human outside the bounds of law, and even outside the bounds of the military tribunal itself, makes that human into the state's possession, infinitely detainable. What counts as "dangerous" is what is deemed dangerous by the state, so that, once again, the state posits what is dangerous, and in so positing it, establishes the conditions for its own preemption and usurpation of the law, a notion of law that has already been usurped by a tragic facsimile of a trial.

If a person is simply deemed dangerous, then it is no longer a matter of deciding whether criminal acts occurred. Indeed, "deeming" someone dangerous is an unsubstantiated judgment that in these cases works to preempt determinations for which evidence is required. The license to brand and categorize and detain on the basis of suspicion alone, expressed in this operation of "deeming," is potentially enormous. We have already seen it at work in racial profiling, in the detention of thousands of Arab residents or Arab-American citizens, sometimes on the basis of last names alone; the harassment of any number of US and non-US citizens at the immigration borders because some official "perceives" a potential difficulty; the attacks on individuals of Middle Eastern descent on US streets, and the targeting of Arab-American professors on campuses. When Rumsfeld has sent the US into periodic panics or "alerts," he has not told the population what to look out for, but only to have a heightened awareness of suspicious activity. This objectless panic translates too quickly into suspicion of all dark-skinned peoples, especially those who are Arab, or appear to look so to a population not always well versed in making visual distinctions, say, between Sikhs and Muslims or, indeed, Sephardic or Arab Jews and Pakistani-Americans. Although "deeming" someone dangerous is considered a state prerogative in these discussions, it is also a potential license for prejudicial perception and a virtual mandate to heighten racialized ways of looking and judging in the name of national security. A population of Islamic peoples, or those taken to be Islamic, has become targeted by this government mandate to be on heightened alert, with the effect that the Arab population in the US becomes visually rounded up, stared down, watched, hounded and monitored by a group of citizens who understand themselves as foot soldiers in the war against terrorism. What kind of public culture is being created when a certain "indefinite containment" takes place outside the prison walls, on the subway, in the airports, on the street, in the workplace? A falafel restaurant run by Lebanese Christians that does not exhibit the American flag becomes immediately suspect, as if the failure to fly the flag in the months following September 11, 2001 were a sign of sympathy with al-Qaeda, a deduction that has no justification, but which nevertheless ruled public culture—and business interests—at that time.

If it is the person, or the people, who are deemed dangerous, and no dangerous acts need to be proven to establish this as true, then the state constitutes the detained population unilaterally, taking them out of the jurisdiction of the law, depriving them of the legal protections to which subjects under national and international law are entitled. These are surely populations that are not regarded as subjects, humans who are not conceptualized within the frame of a political culture in which human lives are underwritten by legal entitlements, law, and so humans who are not humans.

We saw evidence for this derealization of the human in the photos of the shackled bodies in Guantanamo released by the Department of Defense. The DOD did not hide these photos, but published them openly. My speculation is that they published these photographs to make known that a certain vanquishing had taken place, the reversal of national humiliation, a sign of a successful vindication. These were not photographs leaked to the press by some human rights agency or concerned media enterprise. So the international response was no doubt disconcerting, since instead of moral triumph, many people, British parliamentarians and European human rights activists among them, saw serious moral failure. Instead of vindication, many saw instead revenge, cruelty, and a nationalist and self-satisfied flouting of international convention. So that several countries asked that their citizens be returned home for trial.

But there is something more in this degradation that calls to be read. There is a reduction of these human beings to animal status, where the animal is figured as out of control, in need of total restraint. It is important to remember that the bestialization of the human in this way has little, if anything, to do with actual animals, since it is a figure of the animal against which the human is defined. Even if, as seems most probable, some or all of these people have violent intentions, have been engaged in violent acts, and murderous ones, there are ways to deal with murderers under both criminal and international law. The language with which they are described by the US, however, suggests that these individuals are exceptional, that they may not be individuals at all, that they must be constrained in order not to kill, that they are effectively reducible to a desire to kill, and that regular criminal and international codes cannot apply to beings such as these.

The treatment of these prisoners is considered as an extension of war itself, not as a postwar question of appropriate trial and punishment. Their detention stops the killing. If they were not detained, and forcibly so when any movement is required, they would apparently start killing on the spot; they are beings who are in a permanent and perpetual war. It may be that al-Qaeda representatives speak this way—some clearly do—but that does not mean that every individual detained embodies that position, or that those detained are centrally concerned with the continuation of war. Indeed, recent reports, even from the investigative team in Guantanamo, suggest that some of the detainees were only tangentially or transiently involved in the war effort.[11] Other reports in the spring of 2003 made clear that some detainees are minors, ranging from ages thirteen to sixteen. Even General Dunlavey, who admitted that not all the detainees were killers, still claimed that the risk is too high to release such detainees. Rumsfeld cited in support of forcible detention the prison uprisings in Afghanistan in which prisoners managed to get hold of weapons and stage a battle inside the prison. In this sense, the war is not, and cannot be, over; there is a chance of battle in the prison, and there is a warrant for physical restraint, such that the postwar prison becomes the continuing site of war. It would seem that the rules that govern combat are in place, but not the rules that govern the proper treatment of prisoners separated from the war itself.

When General Counsel Haynes was asked, "So you could in fact hold these people for years without charging them, simply to keep them off the street, even if you don't charge them?" he replied, "We are within our rights, and I don't think anyone disputes it that we may hold enemy combatants for the duration of the conflict. And the conflict is still going and *we don't see an end in sight right now*" (my emphasis).

If the war is against terrorism, and the definition of terrorism expands to include every questionable instance of global difficulty, how can the war end? Is it, by definition, a war without end, given the lability of the terms "terrorism" and "war"? Although the pictures were published as a sign of US triumph, and so apparently indicating a conclusion to the war effort, it was clear at the time that bombing and armed conflict were continuing in Afghanistan, the war was not over, and even the photographs, the degradation, and the indefinite detention were continuing acts of war. Indeed, war seems to have established a more or less permanent condition of national emergency, and the sovereign right to self-protection outflanks any and all recourse to law.

The exercise of sovereign power is bound up with the extra-legal status of these official acts of speech. These acts become the means by which sovereign power extends itself; the more it can produce equivocation, the more effectively it can augment its power in the apparent service of justice. These official statements are also media performances, a form of state speech that establishes a domain of official utterance distinct from legal discourse. When many organizations and countries questioned whether the US was honoring the Geneva Convention protocols on the treatment of prisoners of war, the administration equivocated in its response. It maintained that the prisoners at Guantanamo were being treated in a manner "consistent with" the Geneva Convention, they did not say that they understand the US to be obligated to honor that law, or that this law has a binding power on the US. The power of the Geneva Convention has been established by the US as nonbinding in several instances over the last few years. The first instance seemed to be the claim that appears to honor the convention, namely, that the US is acting in a manner *consistent with* the convention, or, alternatively, that the US is acting *in the spirit of* the Geneva Accords. To say that the US acts consistently with the accords is to say that the US acts in such a way that does not contradict the accords, but it does not say that the US, as a signatory to the accords, understands itself as *bound to* the accords. To acknowledge the latter would be to acknowledge the limits that international accords impose upon claims of national sovereignty. To act "consistently" with the accords is still to determine one's own action, and to regard that action as compatible with the accords, but to refuse the notion that one's actions are subject to the accords. Matters get worse when we see that certain rights laid out in the Geneva Accords, Article 3, such as a war prisoner's right to counsel, to knowing the crime for which he is being charged, to be eligible for a timely consideration by a regularly constituted court, for rights of appeal, and a timely repatriation, are not being honored and are not in the planning. Matters became even more vexed, but perhaps finally more clear, when we heard that *none* of the detainees in Guantanamo are to be regarded as prisoners of war according to the Geneva Convention, since none of them belong to "regular armies." Under pressure, the Bush administration conceded that the Taliban were covered by the Geneva Convention, because they were the representatives of the Afghan government, but that they are still unentitled to prisoner of war status under that accord. Indeed, the administration finally said quite clearly that the Geneva Accord was not designed to handle this kind of war, and so its stipulations about who is and is not regarded as a prisoner of war, who is entitled to the rights pertaining to such a status, are anachronistic. The administration thus dismisses the accords as anachronistic, but claims to be acting consistently with them.

When relatively widespread outrage emerged in response to the published photographs of the shackled bodies in Guantanamo, the US asserted it was treating these prisoners humanely. The word, "humanely" was used time and again, and in conjunction with the claim that the US was acting consistently with the Geneva Convention. It seems important to recognize that one of the tasks of the Geneva Convention was to establish criteria for determining what does and does not qualify as the humane treatment of prisoners of war. In other words, one of the tasks was to seek to establish an international understanding of "humane treatment" and to stipulate what conditions must first be met before we can say with certainty that humane treatment has been offered. The term "humane treatment" thus received a legal formulation, and the result was a set of conditions which, if satisfied, would constitute humane treatment. When the US says, then, that it is treating these prisoners humanely, it uses the word in its own way and for its own purpose, but it does not accept that the Geneva Accords stipulate how the term might legitimately be applied.[12] In effect, it takes the word back from the accords at the very moment that it claims to be acting consistently with the accords. In the moment that it claims to be acting consistently with the accords, the US effectively maintains that the accords have no power over it. Similarly, if the US claims that it recognizes that the Taliban are to be considered under the Geneva Convention, but then maintains that even Taliban soldiers are not entitled to prisoner of war status, it effectively disputes the binding power of the agreement. Given that the agreement maintains that a competent tribunal must be set up to determine prisoner of war status, and that all prisoners are to be treated as POWs until such time as a competent tribunal makes a different determination, and given that the US has arranged for no such tribunal and has made this determination unilaterally, the US disregards the very terms of the agreement again. As a result, the "recognition" of the Taliban as being covered by an accord that the US treats as non-binding is effectively worthless, especially when it continues to deny POW status to those it ostensibly recognizes.

We can see that the speech acts sound official at the same time as they defy the law; the speech acts make use of the law only to twist and suspend the law in the end, even make use of the law arbitrarily to elaborate the exercise of sovereignty. And it is not that sovereignty exists as a possession that the US is said to "have" or a domain that the US is said "to occupy." Grammar defeats us here. Sovereignty is what is tactically produced through the very mechanism of its self-justification. And that mechanism, in this circumstance, turns again and again on either relegating law to an instrumentality of the state or of suspending law in the interests of the executive function of the state. The US shows contempt for its own constitution and the protocols of international law in relegating law to an instrumentality of the state and suspending law in the interests of the state. When a reporter asked the DOD representatives why a military tribunal system was required, given that both a civil court and a military court system already exist, they responded that they needed another "instrument," given the new circumstances. The law is not that to which the state is subject nor that which distinguishes between lawful state action and unlawful, but is now expressly understood as an instrument, an instrumentality of power, one that can be applied and suspended at will. Sovereignty consists now in the variable application, contortion, and suspension of the law; it is, in its current form, a relation to law: exploitative, instrumental, disdainful, preemptory, arbitrary.

On C-SPAN in February of 2002, Rumsfeld appeared exasperated with the legal questions about Guantanamo which at that time centered on humane treatment and POW status. He repeatedly appealed instead to a substantive military and public goal to justify the treatment of prisoners in Cuba. He leaned over the microphone and exclaimed that he was just trying to keep these people off the streets and out of the nuclear power plants, so that they would not kill any more people—people have to be detained so they do not kill. In answer to the question of whether or not the detainees will be charged with a crime, whether they could expect trials, he thought it was reasonable to expect that they would, but he offered no commitment to that effect. Here again he did not understand the Department of Defense to be obligated in any way to do that in a timely fashion after a conflict is concluded or, indeed, to commit itself to following the international law that would make of that a strict obligation and an unconditional right. It was "perfectly reasonable" to keep them off the streets, he said, so that they do not kill. And so what it seems perfectly reasonable to do is the basis for what he and the government are doing, and the "law" is surely there to be consulted, as international convention is there as a kind of model, but not as an obligatory framework for action. The action is autonomous, outside the law, looking to the law, considering it, consulting it, even perhaps, on occasion, acting consistently with it. But the action is itself extra-legal, and understands itself to be justified as such. In fact, the law seemed to bother him. In responding to all these questions about legal rights and responsibilities, he remarked that he would leave these questions to others who did not drop out of law school, as he had. And then he laughed, as if some praiseworthy evidence of his own American manhood was suddenly made public. The show of strength indifferent to the law was early on encapsulated by Bush's "Dead or Alive" slogan applied to Osama bin Laden, and Rumsfeld seems to continue this cowboy tradition of vigilante justice in the current situation.

He wouldn't worry about the metal sheets that act as roofs on the cages in which the prisoners are found. After all, Rumsfeld said earnestly, I've been to Cuba, and it has beautiful weather. And then, as if these legal questions were so many gnats around his ankle on a hot day in Cuba, he says, "I'm not a lawyer. I'm not into that end of the business."

So he's not into that end of the business, but we might say that, more generally, many actions have been taken that are not into that end of the business. Bush expressed this sentiment a few days later by claiming with an air of disdain and exasperation that he would review all the "legalisms" before making a final decision on their status. At work in these statements is the presumption that detention and legal process are separable activities, that detention is the DOD's end of the business, and legal processes belong somewhere else. So the question is whether these are illegal combatants, those who are not fighting in a regular armed force, as the US maintains, or whether this is illegal detention, as international rights perspectives seem to concur that it is. It is as if the entire conflict takes place in an extra-legal sphere or, rather, that the extra-legal domain in which these detentions and expected trials take place produces an experience of the "as if" that deals a blow to the common understanding of law. The confusion Rumsfeld had—and here it is not just a matter of his confusion, but a confusion that runs through the entire detainment effort—when asked whether these people had been charged with anything is telling: "Well, yes," he said, hesitating; "they have been charged," and then, as if realizing that this term might have a technical meaning, he revised his claim, explaining that they "have been *found to be* people shooting," emphasizing the word "found." Of course, they haven't been "found" in some legal sense, but only "found" by someone, a representative of the Northern Alliance most likely, who claimed to see or to know, and so a certain equivocation takes place between a legal and non-legal use of "a finding." The fact remains that these individuals are being detained without having been charged with a crime or given access to lawyers to prepare their own cases. That there are rules governing lawful detention of war prisoners does not seem to be important. Of importance, apparently, is averting the consequence of having potential killers on the street. If the law gets in the way, if the law requires that charges be made and substantiated within a given period of time, then there is a chance that compliance with the law would stand in the way of realizing the goal of the more or less permanent detention of "suspects" in the name of national security.

So, these prisoners, who are not prisoners, will be tried, if they will be tried, according to rules that are not those of a constitutionally defined US law nor of any recognizable international code. Under the Geneva Convention, the prisoners would be entitled to trials under the same procedures as US soldiers, through court martial or civilian courts, and not through military tribunals as the Bush administration has proposed. The current regulations for military tribunals provide for the death penalty if all members of the tribunal agree to it. The President, however, will be able to decide on that punishment unilaterally in the course of the final stage of deliberations in which an executive judgment is made and closes the case. Is there a timeframe set forth in which this particular judicial operation will cease to be? In response to a reporter who asked whether the government was not creating procedures that would be in place indefinitely, "as an ongoing additional judicial system created by the executive branch," General Counsel Haynes pointed out that the "the rules [for the tribunals] ... do not have a sunset provision in them ... I'd only observe that the war, we think, will last for a while."

One might conclude with a strong argument that government policy ought to follow established law. And in a way, that is part of what I am calling for. But there is also a problem with the law, since it leaves open the possibility of its own retraction, and, in the case of the Geneva Convention, extends "universal" rights only to those imprisoned combatants who belong to "recognizable" nation-states, but not to all people. Recognizable nation-states are those that are already signatories to the convention itself. This means that stateless peoples or those who belong to states that are emergent or "rogue" or generally unrecognized lack all protections. The Geneva Convention is, in part, a civilizational discourse, and it nowhere asserts an entitlement to protection against degradation and violence and rights to a fair trial as universal rights. Other international covenants surely do, and many human rights organizations have argued that the Geneva Convention can and ought to be read to apply universally. The

International Committee of the Red Cross made this point publicly (February 8, 2002). Kenneth Roth, Director of Human Rights Watch, has argued strongly that such rights do pertain to the Guantanamo Prisoners (January 28, 2002), and the Amnesty International Memorandum to the US Government (April 15, 2002), makes clear that fifty years of international law has built up the assumption of universality, codified clearly in Article 9(4) of the International Covenant on Civil and Political Rights, ratified by the US in 1992. Similar statements have been made by the International Commission on Jurists (February 7, 2002) and the Organization for American States human rights panel made the same claim (March 13, 2002), seconded by the Center for Constitutional Rights (June 10, 2002). Exclusive recourse to the Geneva Convention, itself drafted in 1949, as the document for guidance in this area is thus in itself problematic. The notion of "universality" embedded in that document is restrictive in its reach: it counts as subjects worthy of protection only those who belong already to nation-states recognizable within its terms. In this way, then, the Geneva Convention is in the business of establishing and applying a selective criterion to the question of who merits protection under its provisions, and who does not. The Geneva Convention assumes that certain prisoners may *not* be protected by its statute. By clearly privileging those prisoners from wars between recognizable states, it leaves the stateless unprotected, and it leaves those from non-recognized polities without recourse to its entitlements.

Indeed, to the extent that the Geneva Convention gives grounds for a distinction between legal and illegal combatants, it distinguishes between legitimate and illegitimate violence. Legitimate violence is waged by recognizable states or "countries," as Rumsfeld puts it, and illegitimate violence is precisely that which is committed by those who are landless, stateless, or whose states are deemed not worth recognizing by those who are already recognized. In the present climate, we see the intensification of this formulation as various forms of political violence are called "terrorism," not because there are valences of violence that might be distinguished from one another, but as a way of characterizing violence waged by, or in the name of, authorities deemed illegitimate by established states. As a result, we have the sweeping dismissal of the Palestinian Intifada as "terrorism" by Ariel Sharon, whose use of state violence to destroy homes and lives is surely extreme. The use of the term, "terrorism," thus works to delegitimate certain forms of violence committed by non-state-centered political entities at the same time that it sanctions a violent response by established states. Obviously, this has been a tactic for a long time as colonial states have sought to manage and contain the Palestinians and the Irish Catholics, and it was also a case made against the African National Congress in apartheid South Africa. The new form that this kind of argument is taking, and the naturalized status it assumes, however, will only intensify the enormously damaging consequences for the struggle for Palestinian self-determination. Israel takes advantage of this formulation by holding itself accountable to no law at the very same time that it understands itself as engaged in legitimate self-defense by virtue of the status of its actions as state violence. In this sense, the framework for conceptualizing global violence is such that "terrorism" becomes the name to describe the violence of the illegitimate, whereas legal war becomes the prerogative of those who can assume international recognition as legitimate states.

The fact that these prisoners are seen as pure vessels of violence, as Rumsfeld claimed, suggests that they do not become violent for the same kinds of reason that other politicized beings do, that their violence is somehow constitutive, groundless, and infinite, if not innate. If this violence is terrorism rather than violence, it is conceived as an action with no political goal, or cannot be read politically. It emerges, as they say, from fanatics, extremists, who do not espouse a point of view, but rather exist outside of "reason," and do not have a part in the human community. That it is Islamic extremism or terrorism simply means that the dehumanization that Orientalism already performs is heightened to an extreme, so that the uniqueness and exceptionalism of this kind of war makes it exempt from the presumptions and protections of universality and civilization. When the very human status of those who are imprisoned is called into question, it is a sign that we have made use of a certain parochial frame for understanding the human, and failed to expand our conception of human rights to include those whose values may well test the limits of our own. The figure of Islamic extremism is a very reductive one at this point in time, betraying an extreme ignorance about the various social and political forms that Islam takes, the tensions, for instance, between Sunni and Shiite Muslims, as well as the wide range of religious practices that have few, if any, political implications such as the *da'wa* practices of the mosque movement, or whose political implications are pacifist.

If we assume that everyone who is human goes to war like us, and that this is part of what makes them recognizably human, or that the violence we commit is violence that falls within the realm of the recognizably human, but the violence that others commit is unrecognizable as human activity, then we make use of a limited and limiting cultural frame to understand what it is to be human. This is no reason to dismiss the term "human," but only a reason to ask how it works, what it forecloses, and what it sometimes opens up. To be human implies many things, one of which is that we are the kinds of beings who must live in a world where clashes of value do and will occur, and that these clashes are a sign of what a human community is. How we handle those conflicts will also be a sign of our human-ness, one that is, importantly, in the making. *Whether or not we*

continue to enforce a universal conception of human rights at moments
of outrage and incomprehension, precisely when we think that others
have taken themselves out of the human community as we know it, is a
test of our very humanity. We make a mistake, therefore, if we take
a single definition of the human, or a single model of rationality, to
be the defining feature of the human, and then extrapolate from
that established understanding of the human to all of its various
cultural forms. That direction will lead us to wonder whether some
humans who do not exemplify reason and violence in the way defined
by our definition are still human, or whether they are "exceptional"
(Haynes) or "unique" (Hastert), or "really bad people" (Cheney)
presenting us with a limit case of the human, one in relation to which
we have so far failed. To come up against what functions, for some,
as a limit case of the human is a challenge to rethink the human. And
the task to rethink the human is part of the democratic trajectory of
an evolving human rights jurisprudence. It should not be surprising
to find that there are racial and ethnic frames by which the
recognizably human is currently constituted. One critical operation
of any democratic culture is to contest these frames, to allow a set of
dissonant and overlapping frames to come into view, to take up the
challenges of cultural translation, especially those that emerge when
we find ourselves living in proximity with those whose beliefs and
values challenge our own at very fundamental levels. More crucially,
it is not that "we" have a common idea of what is human, for
Americans are constituted by many traditions, including Islam in
various forms, so any radically democratic self-understanding will
have to come to terms with the heterogeneity of human values. This
is not a relativism that undermines universal claims; it is the condition
by which a concrete and expansive conception of the human will be
articulated, the way in which parochial and implicitly racially and
religiously bound conceptions of human will be made to yield to a

wider conception of how we consider who we are as a global community. We do not yet understand all these ways, and in this sense human rights law has yet to understand the full meaning of the human. It is, we might say, an ongoing task of human rights to reconceive the human when it finds that its putative universality does not have universal reach.

The question of who will be treated humanely presupposes that we have first settled the question of who does and does not count as a human. And this is where the debate about Western civilization and Islam is not merely or only an academic debate, a misbegotten pursuit of Orientalism by the likes of Bernard Lewis and Samuel Huntington who regularly produce monolithic accounts of the "East," contrasting the values of Islam with the values of Western "civilization." In this sense, "civilization" is a term that works against an expansive conception of the human, one that has no place in an internationalism that takes the universality of rights seriously. The term and the practice of "civilization" work to produce the human differentially by offering a culturally limited norm for what the human is supposed to be. It is not just that some humans are treated as humans, and others are dehumanized; it is rather that dehumanization becomes the condition for the production of the human to the extent that a "Western" civilization defines itself over and against a population understood as, by definition, illegitimate, if not dubiously human.

A spurious notion of civilization provides the measure by which the human is defined at the same time that a field of would-be humans, the spectrally human, the deconstituted, are maintained and detained, made to live and die within that extra-human and extra-juridical sphere of life. It is not just the inhumane treatment of the Guantanamo prisoners that attests to this field of beings apprehended, politically, as unworthy of basic human entitlements. It is also found in some of the legal frameworks through which we might

seek accountability for such inhuman treatment, such that the
brutality is continued—revised and displaced—in, for instance, the
extra-legal procedural antidote to the crime. We see the operation of
a capricious proceduralism outside of law, and the production of the
prison as a site for the intensification of managerial tactics untethered
to law, and bearing no relation to trial, to punishment, or to the rights
of prisoners. We see, in fact, an effort to produce a secondary judicial
system and a sphere of non-legal detention that effectively produces
the prison itself as an extra-legal sphere maintained by the extra-
judicial power of the state.

This new configuration of power requires a new theoretical
framework or, at least, a revision of the models for thinking power
that we already have at our disposal. The fact of extra-legal power is
not new, but the mechanism by which it achieves its goals under
present circumstances is singular. Indeed, it may be that this singu-
larity consists in the way the "present circumstance" is transformed
into a reality indefinitely extended into the future, controlling not
only the lives of prisoners and the fate of constitutional and
international law, but also the very ways in which the future may or
may not be thought.

How then finally are we to understand this extra-legal operation
of power? I suggested earlier that the protocols governing indefinite
detention and the new military tribunals reinstitute forms of
sovereign power at both the executive and managerial levels. If the
chronology of modern power that Foucault relays and disputes in his
essay "Governmentality" implies that sovereignty is for the most part
supplanted by governmentality, then the current configuration of
power forces us to rethink the chronology that underwrites that
distinction, as he also suggested we must do. Moreover, if state power
now seeks to instate a sovereign form for itself through the
suspension of the rule of law, it does not follow that the state ceases

to manufacture law. On the contrary, it means only that the law it manufactures, in the form of new military tribunals, is widely considered illegitimate by national and international critics alike.[13] So it is not simply that governmentality becomes a new site for the elaboration of sovereignty, or that the new courts become fully lawless, but that sovereignty trumps established law, and the unaccountable subjects become invested with the task of the discretionary fabrication of law.

This contemporary resurgence of sovereignty is distinct from its other historical operations, but remains tied to them in certain important ways. In "Governmentality" Foucault distinguishes between *the art of government*, which has as its task the management and cultivation of populations, goods, and economic matters, and *the problem of sovereignty*, which, he maintains, is traditionally separated from the management of goods and persons, and is concerned above all with preserving principality and territory. Indeed, sovereignty, as Foucault sketches its evolution from the sixteenth century onwards, comes to have *itself* as its highest aim. He writes, "In every case, what characterizes the end of sovereignty, this common and general good, is in sum nothing other than the submission to sovereignty. This means that the end of sovereignty is circular: this means that the end of sovereignty is the exercise of sovereignty" (95). He calls this the "self-referring circularity of sovereignty" from which it follows that sovereignty's main aim is the positing of its own power. Sovereignty's highest aim is to maintain that very positing power as authoritative and effective. For Machiavelli, Foucault argues, the primary aim of the prince was to "retain his principality" (95). The more contemporary version of sovereignty has to do with the effective exercise of its own power, the positing of itself as sovereign power. We might read the animated traces of this sovereignty in the acts by which officials "deem" a given prisoner to deserve indefinite detention, or the acts by which the executive "deems" a given prisoner to be worthy of a trial, or the acts by which the President decides final guilt or innocence, and whether the death penalty ought to be applied.

Foucault distinguishes governmentality from sovereignty by claiming that governmentality is an art of managing things and persons, concerned with tactics, not laws, or as that which uses laws as part of a broader scheme of tactics to achieve certain policy aims (95). Sovereignty, in its self-referentiality provides a legitimating ground for law, but is for that reason not the same as the law whose legitimacy it is said to underwrite. Indeed, if we take this last point seriously, it would seem that governmentality works to disrupt sovereignty inasmuch as governmentality exposes law as a set of tactics. Sovereignty, on the other hand, seeks to supply the ground for law with no particular aim in sight other than to show or exercise the self-grounding power of sovereignty itself: law is grounded in something other than itself, in sovereignty, but sovereignty is grounded in nothing besides itself.

For Foucault, then, governmentality regards laws as tactics; their operation is "justified" through their aim, but not through recourse to any set of prior principles or legitimating functions. Those functions may be in place, but they are not finally what animates the field of governmentality. Understood in this way, the operations of governmentality are for the most part extra-legal without being illegal. When law becomes a tactic of governmentality, it ceases to function as a legitimating ground: *governmentality makes concrete the understanding of power as irreducible to law*. Thus governmentality becomes the field in which resurgent sovereignty can rear its anachronistic head, for sovereignty is also ungrounded in law. In the present instance, sovereignty denotes a form of power that is fundamentally lawless, and whose lawlessness can be found in the way in which law itself is fabricated or suspended at the will of a designated subject. The new war prison literally manages populations, and thus functions as an operation of governmentality. At the same time, however, it exploits the extra-legal dimension of governmentality to assert a lawless sovereign power over life and death. In other words, the new war prison constitutes a form of governmentality that considers itself its own justification and seeks to extend that self-justificatory form of sovereignty through animating and deploying the extra-legal dimension of governmentality. After all, it will be "officials" who deem suspected terrorists or combatants "dangerous" and it will be "officials," not representatives of courts bound by law, who ostensibly will review the cases of those detained indefinitely. Similarly, the courts themselves are conceived explicitly as "an instrument" used in the service of national security, the protection of principality, the continuing and augmented exercise of state sovereignty.

Foucault casts doubt on a progressive history in which governmentality comes to supplant sovereignty in time, and argues at one point that the two together, along with discipline, have to be understood as contemporary with each other. But what form does sovereignty take once governmentality is established? Foucault offers a narrative in which governmentality supports the continuation of the state in a way that sovereignty no longer can. He writes, for instance, "the art of government only develops once the question of sovereignty ceases to be central" (97). The question of sovereignty seems to be the question of its legitimating function. When this question ceases to be asked, presumably because no answer is forthcoming, the problem of legitimacy becomes less important than the problem of effectivity. The state may or may not be legitimate, or derive its legitimacy from a principle of sovereignty, but it continues to "survive" as a site of power by virtue of governmentalization: the management of health, of prisons, of education, of armies, of goods, along with providing the discursive and institutional conditions for producing and maintaining populations in relation to these. When Foucault writes that "the tactics of governmentality ... make possible the continual definition and redefinition of what is within the competence of the state and what is not," he avows the dependency of the state—its operation as effective power—on governmentality: "The state can only be understood in its survival and its limits on the basis of the general tactics of governmentality" (103). For us, then, the question is: how does the production of a space for unaccountable prerogatory power function as part of the general tactics of governmentality? In other words, under what conditions does governmentality produce a lawless sovereignty as part of its own operation of power?

Foucault argues that the extra-legal sphere of governmentality emerges only once it becomes separated from the "rights of sovereignty." In this sense, then, governmentality depends upon "the question of sovereignty" no longer predominating over the field of power. He argues that "the problem of sovereignty was never posed with greater force than at this time, because it no longer involved ... an attempt to derive an art of government from a theory of sovereignty" (101). Indeed, it appears that once a sphere of managing populations outside of law emerges, sovereignty no longer operates as a principle that would furnish the justification for those forms of population management. What is the use of sovereignty at this point? The self-referring circularity of sovereignty is heightened once this separation of governmentality from sovereignty takes place. It offers no ground, it has no ground, so it becomes radically, if not manically and tautologically, self-grounding in an effort to maintain and extend its own power. But if the self-preserving and self-augmenting aims of the state are once more linked with "sovereignty" (delinked now from the question of its legitimating function), it can be mobilized as one of the tactics of governmentality both to manage populations, to preserve the national state, and to do both while suspending the question of legitimacy. Sovereignty becomes the means by which claims to legitimacy function tautologically.

Although I cannot within the confines of the present analysis consider the various historical ramifications of Foucault's argument, one can see that the present circumstance demands a revision of his theory. It cannot be right, as he claims, that "if the problems of governmentality and the techniques of government have become the only political issues, the only real space for political struggle and contestation, this is because the governmentalization of the state has permitted the state to survive" (103). It is unclear precisely what the relation of state to sovereignty and governmentality is in this formulation, but it seems clear that, however conditioned sovereignty may be, it still drives and animates the state in some important respects. It may be, as Foucault maintains, that governmentality cannot be derived from sovereignty, that whatever causal links once seemed plausible no longer do. But this does not preclude the possibility that governmentality might become the site for the reanimation of that lost ground, the reconstellation of sovereignty in new form. What we have before us now is the deployment of sovereignty as a tactic, a tactic that produces its own effectivity as its aim. Sovereignty becomes that instrument of power by which law is either used tactically or suspended, populations are monitored, detained, regulated, inspected, interrogated, rendered uniform in their actions, fully ritualized and exposed to control and regulation in their daily lives. The prison presents the managerial tactics of governmentality in an extreme mode. And whereas we expect the prison to be tied to law— to trial, to punishment, to the rights of prisoners—we see presently an effort to produce a secondary judicial system and a sphere of non-legal detention that effectively produces the prison itself as an extra-legal sphere. Even if one were tempted to declare that sovereignty is an anachronistic mode of power, one would be forced to come to grips with the means by which anachronisms recirculate within new constellations of power. One might claim that sovereignty is concerned exclusively with a self-grounding exercise and has no instrumental aims, but that would be to underestimate the way that its self-grounding power might be instrumentalized within a broader set of tactics. Sovereignty's aim is to continue to exercise and augment its power to exercise itself; in the present circumstance, however, it can only achieve this aim through managing populations outside the law. So, even as governmental tactics give rise to this sovereignty, sovereignty comes to operate on the very field of governmentality: the management of populations. Finally, it seems important to recognize that one way of "managing" a population is to constitute them as the less than human without entitlement to rights, as the humanly unrecognizable. This is different from producing a subject who is compliant with the law; and it is different from the production of the subject who takes the norm of humanness to be its constitutive principle. The subject who is no subject is neither alive nor dead, neither fully constituted as a subject nor fully deconstituted in death. "Managing" a population is thus not only a process through which regulatory power produces a set of subjects. It is also the process of their de-subjectivation, one with enormous political and legal consequences.

It may seem that the normative implication of my analysis is that I wish the state were bound to law in a way that does not treat the law merely as instrumental or dispensable. This is true. But I am not interested in the rule of law *per se*, however, but rather in the place of law in the articulation of an international conception of rights and obligations that limit and condition claims of state sovereignty. And I am further interested in elaborating an account of power that will produce effective sites of intervention in the dehumanizing effects of the new war prison. I am well aware that international models can be exploited by those who exercise the power to use them to their advantage, but I think that a new internationalism must nevertheless strive for the rights of the stateless, and for forms of self-determination that do not resolve into capricious and cynical forms of state sovereignty. There are advantages to conceiving power in such a way that it is not centered in the nation-state, but conceived, rather, to operate as well through non-state institutions and discourses, since the points of intervention have proliferated, and the aim of politics is not only or merely the overthrow of the state. A broader set of tactics are opened up by the field of governmentality, including those discourses that shape and deform what we mean by "the human."

I am in favor of self-determination as long we understand that no "self," including no national subject, exists apart from an inter-national socius. A mode of self-determination for any given people, regardless of current state status, is not the same as the extra-legal exercise of sovereignty for the purposes of suspending rights at random. As a result, there can be no legitimate exercise of self-determination that is not conditioned and limited by an international conception of human rights that provides the obligatory framework for state action. I am, for instance, in favor of Palestinian self-determination, and even Palestinian statehood, but that process would have to take place supported by, and limited by, international human rights. Similarly, I am equally passionate about Israel giving up religion as a prerequisite for the entitlements of citizenship, and believe that no contemporary democracy can and ought to base itself on exclusionary conditions of participation, such as religion. The Bush administration has broken numerous international treaties in the last two years, many of them having to do with arms control and trade, and many of these abrogations took place prior to the events of September 11. Even the US's call for an international coalition after those events was one that presumed that the US would set the terms, lead the way, determine the criterion for membership, and lead its allies. This is a form of sovereignty that seeks to absorb and instrumentalize an international coalition, rather than submit to a self-limiting practice by virtue of its international obligations. Similarly, Palestinian self-determination will be secured as a right only if there is an international consensus that there are rights to be enforced in the face of a bloated and violent exercise of sovereign prerogative on the part of Israel. My fear is that the indefinite detainment of prisoners on Guantanamo, for whom no rights of appeal will be possible within federal courts, will become a model for the branding and management of so-called terrorists in various global sites where no rights of appeal to international rights and to international courts will be presumed. If this extension of lawless and illegitimate power takes place, we will see the resurgence of a violent and self-aggrandizing state sovereignty at the expense of any commitment to global co-operation that might support and radically redistribute rights of recognition governing who may be treated according to standards that ought to govern the treatment of humans. We have yet to become human, it seems, and now that prospect seems even more radically imperiled, if not, for the time being, indefinitely foreclosed.

4

THE CHARGE OF ANTI-SEMITISM: JEWS, ISRAEL, AND THE RISKS OF PUBLIC CRITIQUE

Profoundly anti-Israeli views are increasingly finding support in progressive intellectual communities. Serious and thoughtful people are advocating and taking actions that are anti-Semitic in their effect if not their intent.

Lawrence Summers, President of Harvard University,
September 17, 2002

When the President of Harvard University, Lawrence Summers, remarked that to criticize Israel at this time and to call upon universities to divest from Israel are "actions that are anti-Semitic in their effect, if not their intent,"[1] he introduced a distinction between an effective and intentional anti-Semitism that is controversial at best. Of course, the counter-charge has been that, in making his statement, the President of Harvard has struck a blow against academic freedom, in effect, if not in intent. Although he himself made clear that he meant nothing censorious by his action, and that he is in favor of these ideas being "debated freely and civilly,"[2] his words nevertheless exercise a chilling effect on political discourse, stoking the fear that to criticize Israel during this time is to expose oneself to the charge of anti-Semitism. He made his claim in relation to several actions which he called "effectively anti-Semitic" which included European boycotts of Israel, anti-globalization rallies in which criticisms of Israel were voiced, and fund-raising efforts for organizations with "questionable political provenance." Of local concern to him, however, was a divestment petition drafted by MIT and Harvard professors who oppose the current Israeli occupation and the treatment of Palestinians. Engaging with this initiative critically, Summers asked why Israel was being "singled out ... among all nations" for a divestment campaign, suggesting that the singling-out was evidence of an anti-Semitic aim. And though Summers claimed that aspects of Israeli policy "can be and should be vigorously challenged," it was unclear how such challenges could or would take place without being construed in some sense as anti-Israel, and why those foreign policy issues, which include "occupation" and are, therefore, given the dispute over legitimate state boundaries, domestic policies as well, ought not to be vigorously challenged through a divestment campaign. It would seem that calling for divestment is something other than a legitimately "vigorous challenge," but we are not given any criteria by which to adjudicate the difference between those vigorous challenges that should be articulated, and those which carry the "effective" force of anti-Semitism.

Of course, Summers is right to voice concern about rising anti-Semitism, and every progressive Jew, along with every progressive person, ought to be vigorously challenging anti-Semitism wherever it occurs, especially if it occurs in the context of movements mobilized in part or in whole against the Israeli occupation of Palestinian lands. It seems, though, that historically we are now in the position in which Jews cannot be understood always and only as presumptive victims. Sometimes we surely are, but sometimes we surely are not. No political ethics can start with the assumption that Jews monopolize the position of victim.[3] The "victim" is a quickly transposable term, and it can shift from minute to minute from the Jew atrociously killed by suicide bombers on a bus to the Palestinian child atrociously killed by Israeli gunfire. The public sphere needs to be one in which *both* kinds of violence are challenged insistently and in the name of justice.

If we think, though, that to criticize Israeli violence, or to call for specific tactics that will put economic pressure on the Israeli state to change its policies, is to engage in "effective anti-Semitism," we will fail to voice our opposition out of fear of being named as part of an anti-Semitic enterprise. No label could be worse for a Jew. The very idea of it puts fear in the heart of any Jew who knows that, ethically and politically, the position with which it would be utterly unbearable to identify is that of the anti-Semite. It recalls images of the Jewish collaborators with the Nazis. And it is probably fair to say that for most progressive Jews who carry the legacy of the Shoah in their psychic and political formations, the ethical framework within which we operate takes the form of the following question: will we be silent (and be a collaborator with illegitimately violent power), or will we make our voices heard (and be counted among those who did what they could to stop illegitimate violence), even if speaking poses a risk to ourselves. The Jewish effort to criticize Israel during these times emerges, I would argue, precisely from this ethos. And though the critique is often portrayed as insensitive to Jewish suffering, in the past and in the present, its ethic is wrought precisely from that experience of suffering, so that suffering itself might stop, so that something we might reasonably call *the sanctity of life* might be honored equitably and truly. The fact of enormous suffering does not warrant revenge or legitimate violence, but must be mobilized in the service of a politics that seeks to diminish suffering universally, that seeks to recognize the sanctity of life, of all lives.

Summers mobilizes the use of the "anti-Semitic" charge to quell public criticism, even as he explicitly distances himself from the overt operations of censorship. He writes, for instance, "The only antidote to dangerous ideas is strong alternatives vigorously defended." But with what difficulty does one vigorously defend the idea that the Israeli occupation is brutal and wrong, and that Palestinian self-determination is a necessary good, if the voicing of those views calls down upon itself the horrible charge of anti-Semitism?

Let us consider his statement in detail, then, in order both to understand what he means and what follows logically from what he has said. In order to understand Summers's claim, we have to be able to conceive of an "effective anti-Semitism," one that pertains to certain kinds of speech acts, which either follows upon certain utterances, or is said to structure those utterances, even if it is not part of the conscious intention of those who make the utterance itself. His view assumes that such utterances will be taken up by others as anti-Semitic, or will be received within a given context as anti-Semitic. If his claim is true, then there will be one way or, perhaps, a predominant way of receiving them, and that will be to receive them as anti-Semitic arguments or utterances. So it seems we have to ask what context Summers has in mind when he makes his claim; in what world, in other words, is it the case that any criticism of Israel will be taken to be anti-Semitic.

Now, it may be that what Summers was effectively saying is that, as a community, largely understood as the public sphere of the US, or, indeed, of a broader international community which might include parts of Europe and parts of Israel, the only way that a criticism of Israel can be heard is through a certain kind of acoustic frame, such that the criticism, whether it is of West Bank settlements, the closing of Birzeit University, the demolition of homes in Ramallah or Jenin, or the killing of numerous children and civilians, can only be taken up and interpreted as an act of hatred for Jews. If we imagine who is listening, and who is hearing the former kinds of criticisms *as* anti-Semitic, that is, expressing hatred for Jews or calling for discriminatory action against Jews, then we are asked to conjure a listener who attributes intention to the speaker: "so and so" has made a public statement against the Israeli occupation of Palestinian territories, and this must mean that "so and so" actually hates Jews or is willing to fuel those who do. The criticism is thus not taken for its face value, but given a hidden meaning, one that is at odds with its explicit claim. In this way, the explicit claim does not have to be heard, since what one is hearing is the hidden claim made beneath the explicit one. The criticism against Israel that is levied is nothing more than a cloak for that hatred, or a cover for a call, transmuted in form, for discriminatory action against Jews.

So whereas Summers himself introduces a distinction between intentional and effective anti-Semitism, it would seem that effective anti-Semitism can be understood only by conjuring a seamless world of listeners and readers who take certain statements critical of Israel to be tacitly or overtly *intended* as anti-Semitic expression. The only way to understand *effective* anti-Semitism would be to presuppose *intentional* anti-Semitism. The effective anti-Semitism of any criticism of Israel will turn out to reside in the intention of the speaker as it is retrospectively attributed by the one who receives— listens to or reads—that criticism. The intention of a speech, then, does not belong to the one who speaks, but is attributed to that speaker later by the one who listens. The intention of the speech act is thus determined belatedly by the listener.

Now it may be that Summers has another point of view in mind, namely, that critical statements *will be used* by those who have anti-Semitic intent, that such statements will be exploited by those who want not only to see the destruction of Israel but the degradation or devaluation of Jewish people in general. In this case, it would seem that the discourse itself, if allowed into the public sphere, will be taken up by those who seek to use it, not only for a criticism of Israel, but as a way of doing harm to Jews, or expressing hatred for them. Indeed, there is always that risk, a risk that negative comments about the Israeli state will be misconstrued as negative comments about Jews. But to claim that the only meaning that such criticism can have is to be taken up as negative comments about Jews is to attribute to that particular interpretation an enormous power to monopolize the field of reception for that criticism. The argument against letting criticisms of Israel into the public sphere would be that it gives fodder to those with anti-Semitic intentions, and that those who have such intentions will successfully co-opt the criticisms made. Here again, the distinction between effective anti-Semitism and intended anti-Semitism folds, insofar as the only way a statement can become effectively anti-Semitic is if there is, somewhere, an intention to use the statement for anti-Semitic aims, an intention imagined as enormously effective in realizing its aims. Indeed, even if one did believe that criticisms of Israel are by and large heard as anti-Semitic (by Jews, by anti-Semites, by people who could be described as neither), it would then become the responsibility of all of us to change the conditions of reception so that the public might begin to learn a crucial political distinction between a criticism of Israel, on the one hand, and a hatred of Jews, on the other.

A further consideration has to take place here, since Summers himself is making a statement, a strong statement, as president of an institution which assumes its value in part as a symbol of academic prestige in the United States. In his statement, he is saying that he, as a listener, will take any criticism of Israel to be effectively anti-Semitic. Although in making his remarks he claimed that he was not speaking as president of the university, but as a "member of the community," his speech was a presidential address, and it carried weight in the press precisely because he exercised the symbolic authority of his office. And in this respect, he models the listener or reader we have been asked to conjure. If he is the one who is letting the public know that he will take any criticism of Israel to be anti-Semitic, that any criticism of Israel will have that effect *on him* and, so, will be "effectively" anti-Semitic, then he is saying that public discourse itself ought to be constrained in such a way that those critical statements are not uttered. If they are uttered, they will be taken up and interpreted in such a way that they will be considered anti-Semitic. The ones who make those arguments will be understood as engaging in anti-Semitic speech, even hate speech. But here it is important to distinguish between anti-Semitic speech that, say, produces a hostile and threatening environment for Jewish students, racist speech which any university administrator would be obligated to oppose and to regulate, and speech that makes a student politically uncomfortable because it opposes a state or a set of state policies that any student may defend. The latter is a political debate, and if we say that the case of Israel is different because the very identity of the student is bound up with the state of Israel, so that any criticism of Israel is considered an attack on "Israelis" or, indeed, "Jews" in general, then we have "singled out" this form of political allegiance from all the other forms of political allegiance in the world that are open to public disputation, and engaged in the most outrageous form of silencing and "effective" censorship.[4]

Indeed, not only, it seems, will Summers regard such criticisms as anti-Semitic, but he is, by his example, and by the normative status of his utterance, recommending that others regard such utterances that way as well. He is setting a norm for legitimate interpretation. We do not know how he would rule on various cases if they were to reach his desk, but his current utterance gives symbolic authority to the claim that such utterances are impermissible, in the same way that racist utterances are. What is complicated, however, is that his understanding of what constitutes anti-Semitic rhetoric depends upon a very specific and very questionable reading of the field of reception for such speech. He seems, through his statement, to be describing a sociological condition under which speech acts occur and are interpreted, that is, describing the fact that we are living in a world where, for better or worse, criticisms of Israel are simply heard as anti-Semitic. He is, however, also speaking as one who is doing that hearing, and so modeling the very hearing that he describes. In this sense, he is producing a prescription: he knows what effect such statements have, and he is telling us about that effect; they will be taken to be anti-Semitic; he takes them to be anti-Semitic; and in this way, rhetorically, he recommends that others take them to be so as well.

The point is not only that his distinction between effective and intentional anti-Semitism cannot hold, but that the way the distinction collapses in his formulation is precisely what produces the condition under which certain public views are taken to be hate speech, in effect if not in intent. One point Summers did not make is that anything that the Israeli state does in the name of its self-defense is fully legitimate and ought not to be questioned. I do not know whether he approves of all Israeli policies, but let us imagine, for the sake of argument, that he does not. And I do not know whether he has views about, for instance, the destruction of homes and the killing of children in Jenin which, last year, attracted the attention of the United Nations but was not investigated as a human rights violation when Israel refused to let the UN survey the scene. Let us imagine that he objects to those actions and those killings, and that they are among the "foreign policy" issues that he believes ought to be "vigorously challenged." If that is the case, then he would be compelled, under his formulation, not to voice his disapproval, believing, as he does, that the voicing of that disapproval would be construed, effectively, as anti-Semitism. And if he thinks it is possible to voice that disapproval, he has not shown us how it might be voiced in such a way that the allegation of anti-Semitism might be averted.

If one were to decide not to voice a criticism of those killings, for fear that that criticism might be taken as critical of the Jews, say, as a people, or as stoking the fires of anti-Semitism elsewhere, one would be compelled to choose between exercising the right or, indeed, obligation to wage public criticism against forms of violent injustice, on the one hand, and fomenting anti-Semitic sentiment through the exercise of that right, on the other. If Summers did object to such policies, would he censor himself and ask that others do the same?

I do not have the answer to this question, but his logic suggests the following: one could conclude, on the basis of a desire to refrain from strengthening anti-Semitic sentiment and belief, that certain actions of the Israeli state—acts of violence and murder against children and civilians—must not be objected to, must go unremarked and unprotested, and that these acts of violence must be allowed to go on, unimpeded by public protest or outrage, for fear that any protest against them would be tantamount to anti-Semitism, if not anti-Semitism itself.

Now, it is surely possible to argue, as I would and do argue, that all forms of anti-Semitism must be opposed, but it would seem that now we have a serious set of confusions about what forms anti-Semitism takes. Indeed, the actual problem of anti-Semitism is elided here by the strategic way that the charge of anti-Semitism works, which means that when and if the charge ought to be made, it will have been made less robust by its use as a threatened interpellation. Indeed, if the charge of anti-Semitism is used to defend Israel at all costs, then the power of the charge to work against those who demean and discriminate against Jews, who do violence to synagogues in Europe, who wave Nazi flags and support anti-Semitic organizations is radically diluted. Indeed, many critics of Israel now dismiss all claims of anti-Semitism as "trumped up," after having been exposed to the use of the claim as a means to censor political speech, and this produces an insensitivity and refusal to acknowledge existing political realities that is worrisome at best. One reason, then, to oppose the use of the charge of anti-Semitism as a threat and as a means to quell political critique is that the charge must be kept alive as a crucial and effective instrument to combat existing and future anti-Semitism.

Summers, on the other hand, does not tell us why divestment campaigns or other forms of public protest *are* anti-Semitic, if they are. Rather, it seems that "anti-Semitism" functions here as a charge, one that does not correspond to a given kind of action or utterance, but one that is unilaterally conferred by those who fear the consequences of overt criticisms of Israel. According to Summers, there are some forms of anti-Semitism that are characterized retroactively by those who decide upon their status. This means that nothing should be said or done that will be taken to be anti-Semitic by others. But what if the others who are listening are wrong? If we take one form of anti-Semitism to be defined retroactively by those who listen to a certain set of speech acts, or witness a certain set of protests against Israel, then what is left of the possibility of legitimate protest against a given state, either by its own population or by those who live outside those borders? If we say that every time "Israel" is uttered, the speaker really means "Jews," then we have foreclosed in advance the possibility that the speaker really means "Israel."

If we distinguish between anti-Semitism and forms of protest against the Israeli state (or, indeed, right-wing settlers who some-times act independently of the state), acknowledging that sometimes they do, disturbingly, work together, then we stand a chance of understanding that the Jewish population of the world does not conceive of itself as one with the Israeli state in its present form and practice, and that Jews *in Israel* do not conceive of themselves as one with the Israeli state. In other words, the possibility of a substantive Jewish peace movement depends upon (a) a productive and critical distance from the state of Israel (one that can be coupled with a profound investment in what future course it takes), and (b) a clear distinction between anti-Semitism, on the one hand, and forms of protest against the Israeli state based on that critical distance, on the other.

I take it that Summers's view, however, relies on the full and seamless identification of the Jewish people with the state of Israel, not only an "identification" that he makes in coupling the two, but also an "identification" that he assumed to be subjectively adopted by Jews themselves. His view seems to imply a further claim as well, namely, that any criticism of Israel is "anti-Israel" in the sense that the criticism is understood to challenge the right of Israel to exist.[5]

I'll turn to the problem of identification in a moment, but let's first consider the latter claim. A criticism of Israel is not the same as a challenge to Israel's existence, and neither is it the same as an anti-Semitic act, though each could work in tandem with each of the other claims. There are conditions under which it would be possible to say that one leads to the next. A challenge to the right of Israel to exist can only be construed as a challenge to the existence of the Jewish people if one believes that Israel alone is what keeps the Jewish people alive or if one believes that all Jewish people have their sense of perpetuity invested in the state of Israel in its current or traditional forms. Only if we make one of these assumptions, it seems, does the very criticism of Israel function as a challenge to the very survival of the Jews. Of course, one could argue that criticism is essential to any democratic polity, and that those polities that safeguard criticism stand a better chance of surviving than those that do not. Let us imagine, for the sake of argument, that one set of criticisms do challenge the basic presuppositions of the Israeli state, ones that produce differential forms of citizenship, ones that secure the Right to Return for Jews, but not Palestinians, ones that maintain a religious basis for the state itself. For a criticism of Israel to be taken as a challenge to the survival of the Jews or Jewishness itself, we would have to assume not only that "Israel" cannot change in response to legitimate criticisms, but that a more radically democratic Israel would be bad for Jews or for Jewishness. According to this latter belief, criticism itself is not a Jewish value, and this clearly flies in the face not only of long traditions of Talmudic disputation, but of all the religious and cultural sources for openly objecting to injustice and illegitimate violence that have been part of Jewish life for centuries, prior to the formation of the contemporary state of Israel, and alongside it.

So it seems that the very meaning of what it is to be Jewish or, indeed, what "Jewishness" is has undergone a certain reduction in the formulation that Summers provides. Summers has identified Jews with the state of Israel as if they were seamlessly the same, or he has assumed that, psychologically and sociologically, every Jew has such an identification, and that this identification is essential to Jewish identity, an identification without which that identity cannot exist. Only on the basis of such presumptions, then, does it follow that any criticism of Israel strikes against a primary identification that Jews are assumed to have with the state of Israel. But what are we to make of Jews who *dis*identify with Israel or, at least, with the Israeli state (which is not the same as every part of its culture)? Or Jews who identify with Israel (Israeli or not), but do not condone or identify with several of its practices? There is a huge range here: those who are silently ambivalent about how Israel handles itself now, those who are half-articulate about their doubts about the occupation, those who are very strongly opposed to the occupation, but within a Zionist framework, those who would like to see Zionism rethought or, indeed, abandoned, and either do or do not voice their views in public. There are Jews who may have any of the given opinions listed above, but voice them only to their family, or never voice them to their family, or only voice them to their friends, but never in public, or voice them in public, but cannot go home again. Given the extraordinary range of Jewish ambivalence on this topic, ought we not to be suspicious of *any* rhetorical effort to assume an equivalence between Jews and Israel? The argument that *all* Jews have a heartfelt investment in the state of Israel is simply untrue. Some have a heartfelt investment in corned beef sandwiches or in certain Talmudic tales, memories of their grandmother, the taste of borscht or the echoes of the Yiddish theatre. Some care most about Hebrew songs or religious liturgy and rituals. Some have an investment in historical and cultural archives from Eastern Europe or from the Shoah, or in forms of labor activism that are thoroughly secular, though "Jewish" in a substantively social sense. There are sources of American Jewish identification, for instance, in food, in religious ritual, in social service organizations, in diasporic communities, in civil rights and social justice struggles that may exist in relative independence from the question of the status of Israel.

What do we make of Jews, including myself, who are emotionally invested in the state of Israel, critical of its current form, and call for a radical restructuring of its economic and juridical basis precisely because they are so invested? Is it always possible to say that such Jews do not know their own best interest, that such Jews turn against other Jews, that such Jews turn against their own Jewishness? But what if one offers criticism of the Israeli state in the name of one's Jewishness, in the name of justice, precisely because, as it were, such criticisms seem "best for the Jews"? Why wouldn't it always be "best for the Jews" to embrace forms of radical democracy that extend what is "best" to everyone, Jewish or not? I signed one such petition, "Open Letter from American Jews," and there were finally 3,700 of us who, identifiably Jewish, opposed the Israeli occupation.[6] This was a limited criticism, since it did not call for the end of Zionism *per se*, or for the reallocation of arable land, for rethinking the Jewish right of return, or for the fair distribution of water and medicine to Palestinians, and it did not call for the reorganization of the Israeli state on a more radically egalitarian basis. But it was, nevertheless, an overt criticism of Israel. Let us assume that a vast number of those who signed that petition undergo something we might reasonably term *heartache* when taking a stand against Israeli policy in public, and that hands shook as they entered their names on that list. The heartache emerges from the thought that Israel, by subjecting 3.5 million Palestinians to a military occupation, represents the Jews in a way that these petitioners find not only objectionable, but truly terrible to endure, *as Jews*; it is precisely *as Jews*, even in the name of a different Jewish future, that they call for another way, that they assert their disidentification with that policy, they assert another path for Jewish politics, they seek to widen the rift between the state of Israel and the Jewish people to produce an alternative vision. This rift is crucial for opening up and sustaining a critical relation to the state of Israel, its military power, its differential forms of citizenship, its unmonitored practices of torture, its brutality at the borders, and its egregious nationalism.

One could take the psychological view and say that these petitioners suffer from internalized anti-Semitism, but Summers, to be fair, does not make this statement, even if, *effectively*, the statement seems to follow logically from what he does say. If one calls for universities to divest from the state of Israel, as I, along with many others, have done, that is not the same as condoning the position that Israel should be "driven into the sea," and it is not, as a public speech act, tantamount to driving Israel into the sea. The speech act calls upon Israel to embody certain democratic principles, to end the occupation and, in some instances, to reject the Zionist basis of the current state in favor of a more egalitarian and democratic one. The petition exercises a democratic right to voice criticism, and it seeks to impose economic pressure on Israel by the US and other countries to implement rights for Palestinians otherwise deprived of basic conditions of self-determination. The criticisms of Israel can take several different forms, and they differ according to whether they are generated within the state or from the outside: some wish for the implementation of human rights; some wish for the end of the occupation; some call for an independent Palestinian state, and some call to reestablish the basis of the Israeli state itself without regard to religion so that a one-state solution would offer citizenship on an equal basis to all inhabitants of that land. According to this last call, Jewishness would no longer be the basis of the state, but would constitute one multivalent cultural and religious reality in that state, protected by the same laws that protect the rights of religious expression and cultural self-determination of all other people who have claims to that land.[7]

It is important to remember that the identification of Jewishness with Israel, implied by the formulation that maintains that to criticize Israel is effectively to engage in anti-Semitism, elides the reality of a small but dynamic peace movement in Israel itself. What do we make of those who are to the left of Peace Now, who belong to the small, but important post-Zionist movement in Israel, such as the philosophers Adi Ophir and Anat Biletzki, the Professor of Theatre Avraham Oz, the sociologist Uri Ram, or the poet Yitzhak Laor? Are we to say that Jews, nay, Israelis who are critical of Israeli policy or, indeed, call into question the structure and self-legitimating practices of the Israeli state are therefore self-hating Jews, or that they fail to be sensitive to the ways in which these criticisms can fan the flames of anti-Semitism? Could it be instead that these critics hold out a different path for the state of Israel, and that their politics, in fact, emerge from other sources of political vision, some clearly Jewish, than those that have currently been codified as Zionism? What are we to make of the new organization Brit Tzedek in the US, numbering close to 20,000 members on last count, which seeks to offer an alternative American Jewish voice to AIPAC,[8] opposing the current military occupation and struggling for a two-state solution?[9] And what about Jewish Voices for Peace, and Jews Against the Occupation, Jews for Peace in the Middle East, the Faculty for Israeli–Palestinian Peace,[10] Tikkun, Jews for Racial and Economic Justice, Women in Black or, indeed, the critical mission of Neve Shalom—Wahat al-Salam, the only village collectively governed by both Jews and Arabs in the state of Israel, which also houses the School for Peace that offers instruction in conflict resolution that opposes Israeli militaristic strategy.[11] What are we to make of the Israel/Palestine Center for Research and Information in Jerusalem?[12] And what do we make of B'Tselem, the Israeli human rights organization that monitors human rights abuses on the West Bank and in Gaza, or Gush Shalom,[13] the Israeli organization against the occupation, or Yesh Gvul, 2003,[14] the Israeli soldiers who refused to serve in the occupied territories? And, finally, what do we make of Ta'ayush (which means "living together" in Arabic)? This last is a coalition that not only seeks peace in the region, but which, through Jewish–Arab collaborative actions, opposes state policies that lead to isolation, poor medical care, house arrest, the destruction of educational institutions, and a lack of water and food for Palestinians living under the occupation. Let me cite from one member's description of that group sent to me in the fall of 2002, a young literary critic named Catherine Rottenberg:

> It is a grassroots movement which emerged after the October 2000 events—the outbreak of the second intifada and the killing of 13 Arab citizens within Israel. The Israeli peace camp, particularly Peace Now, did nothing to bring people to the streets; in fact, there was barely a murmur of protest. It began when some professors at Tel Aviv University and Palestinian citizens of Israel from Kfar Kassem decided that a new and real Arab–Jewish movement was desperately needed. There were a dozen activists at the time. Now there are Ta'ayush branches all across Israel and about a thousand activists.
>
> Many of us were tired of going to protests to stand—once again—with a sign in our hand …. We were thinking more of resistance than of protest. Basically, we use non-violent civil disobedience to convey our message (which is similar to the one endorsed by the American Jewish academics [see "Open Letter …"]—but more radical). In Israel, we are probably best known for our food and solidarity convoys that defy the military siege, often breaking through physical barriers, not only the psychological ones. Jewish and Palestinian citizens of Israel travel in convoys made up of private cars (our last convoy included approximately a hundred cars) to West Bank villages where we establish—in advance—strong ties through months of dialogue. We try to break the walls —physical, psychological, and political—separating the two

peoples and expose the brutality of the occupation. We bring humanitarian aid, but we use it more as a political tool to break the siege than as humanitarian relief. It doesn't look good in the international press when Israel prevents humanitarian aid from reaching the villages—although it does it all the time!

We usually manage to get some media attention. We have also helped organize many demonstrations; these are always in coalition with other organizations (like the Women's Coalition for a Just Peace).

Yesterday (August, 2002), Ta'ayush tried to reach Bethlehem— to break the curfew and to demonstrate with the residents against Israel's draconian policies. The police didn't let us enter the city, of course, and used tear gas and water hoses to disperse us. But we demonstrated anyway, near the checkpoint, calling our Palestinian partners (in Bethlehem) by cell phone so that they could speak to the crowd.

In the past few months, we have also worked within Israel, trying to expose and fight discrimination against the Palestinian population. Last week we organized a work camp at one of the many unrecognized villages in the North and next week a water convoy will go to unrecognized Bedouin villages that still do not have running water.

I have been an activist for many years, but Ta'ayush is something extraordinary. It has been an amazing learning experience —both in terms of democracy, as well as how to negotiate gender, class, sexuality and race in times of crisis. We all have different political agendas, but we have always managed somehow to maintain dialogue and work together. There is no office, no official positions, it is democracy at work and consequently we have hours and hours and hours of meetings. We have created a real community and as far as I can see, it is the only light (small that it is) at the moment.[15]

Such organizations are not only expressing notions of "Jewish" collectivity, but, like Neve Shalom, undercut a nationalist ethos in the interests of developing a new political basis for coexistence. They are, we might say, diasporic elements working with Israel itself to dislodge the pervasive assumption of nationalism. As Yitzhak Laor remarks, "a joint life means relinquishing parts of a national ethos."[16]

It seems crucial not only for the purposes of academic freedom, but surely for that as well, that we consider these issues carefully, since it will not do to equate Jews with Zionists or, indeed, Jewishness with Zionism. There were debates throughout the nineteenth century and the early twentieth, and indeed at the inception of Israel, among Jews whether Zionism was a legitimate political ideology, whether it ought to become the basis of a state, whether the Jews had any right, understood in a modern sense, to lay claim to that land—land inhabited by Palestinians for centuries—and what future lay ahead for a Jewish political project based upon the violent expropriation of the land of Palestinians, dispossession on a massive scale, slaughter, and the sustained suspension of fundamental rights for Palestinians. There were those who sought to make Zionism compatible with peaceful coexistence, and others who made use of it for military aggression, and still do. There were those who thought, and who still think, that Zionism is not a legitimate basis for a democratic state in a situation where it must be assumed that a diverse population practices different religions, and that no group, on the basis of their ethnic or religious views, ought to be excluded from any right accorded to citizens in general. And there are those who maintain that the violent appropriation of Palestinian lands, and the dislocation of 700,000 Palestinians at the time that Israel was founded has produced a violent and dehumanizing basis for this particular state formation, one which repeats its founding gesture in the containment and dehumanization of Palestinians in the occupied territories. Indeed, the new "wall" being built between Israel and the occupied territories threatens to leave 95,000 Palestinians homeless. These are surely questions and issues to be asked about Zionism that should and must be asked in a public domain, and universities are surely one place where we might depend upon a critical reflection on Zionism to take place. But instead of understanding the topic of "Zionism" to be something worthy of critical and open debate, we are being asked, by Summers and by others, to treat any critical approach to Zionism as "effective anti-Semitism" and, hence, to rule it out as a topic for legitimate disagreement and discussion.

What better time, though, to ask after the history of Zionism, the implications of its implementation, the alternatives that were foreclosed when it took hold in 1948 and before, and what future, if any, it ought to have? A crucial history needs to be uncovered and opened to new debate: what were Hannah Arendt's objections to Zionism, and why did Martin Buber come to disavow its project? What were the movements critical of the Israeli state from its inception from within the community of Jews in Palestine: B'rith Shalom, the Matzpen Movement? In the academy we ask these questions about US traditions of political belief and practice; we consider various forms of socialism critically and openly; and we consider in a wide variety of contexts the problematic nexus of religion and nationalism. What does it mean to paralyze our capacities for critical scrutiny and historical inquiry when this topic becomes the issue, fearing that we will become exposed to the charge of "anti-Semitism" if we utter our worries, our heartache, our objection, our outrage in a public form? To say, effectively, that anyone who utters their heartache and outrage out loud will be considered (belatedly, and by powerful "listeners") as anti-Semitic, is to seek to control the kind of speech that circulates in the public sphere, to terrorize with the charge of anti-Semitism, and to produce a climate of fear through the tactical use of a heinous judgment with which no progressive person would want to identify. If we bury our criticism for fear of being labeled anti-Semitic, we give power to those who want to curtail the free expression of political beliefs. To live with the charge is, of course, terrible, but it is less terrible when you know that it is untrue, and one can only have this knowledge if there are others who are speaking with you, and who can help to support the sense of what you know.

When Daniel Pipes established "Campus Watch" in the fall of 2002, he produced a blacklist of scholars in Middle Eastern Studies who were, in his view, known to be critical of Israel and thus understood to be anti-Semitic or to be fomenting anti-Semitism. An email campaign was begun by Mark Lance, a philosopher at Georgetown University, in which a number of us wrote in to complain about not being listed on the site. The point of the email initiative was to undermine the power of "blacklisting" as a tactic reminiscent of McCarthyism. Most of us wrote in to say that, if believing in Palestinian self-determination was adequate for membership on the list, we wished to be included as well. Although we were subsequently branded as "apologists" for anti-Semitism, and listed on the web under this heading, there were no individuals who were part of this campaign who accepted the notion that to criticize Israel or to promote Palestinian self-determination were anti-Semitic acts. Indeed, when Tamar Lewin from the *New York Times* contacted me after my name was associated with the beginning of this campaign, she said she was doing a story on rising anti-Semitism on campus, implying that the opposition to the Daniel Pipes website was evidence of this rise. I explained to her that I was, like many others who wrote in, a progressive Jew (handling the discourse of identity politics for the moment), and that I rejected the notion that to support Palestinian self-determination was in itself an anti-Semitic act. I referred her to several Jewish organizations and petitions that held views such as my own, and suggested that this was not a story about anti-Semitism, but about how the charge of anti-Semitism plays to silence certain political viewpoints. Her story in the *New York Times*, "Web Site Fuels Debates on Campus Anti-Semitism" (September 27, 2002), skewed the issue significantly since it accepted the assumption that there were "pro-Israel" and "pro-Palestinian" positions that did not have any overlap, and it refused to name as Jewish several of us who opposed the website and its neo-McCarthyism. Indeed, the article managed to associate those who opposed Pipes with anti-Semitism itself, even though we had, in conversation with her, made clear our profound revulsion at anti-Semitism.

So many important distinctions are elided by the mainstream press when it assumes that there are only two positions on the Middle East, and that they can be adequately described by the terms "pro-Israel" and "pro-Palestinian." Various people are said to hold views that are one or the other, and the assumption is that these are discrete views, internally homogeneous, non-overlapping. And the terms suggest that if one is "pro-Israel" then anything Israel does is all right, or if one is "pro-Palestinian" then anything Palestinians do is all right. But true views on the political spectrum do not fall easily into such extremes. So many complex formulations of political belief are erased from view. One can, for instance, be in favor of Palestinian self-determination, but condemn suicide bombings, and still differ with others who share both views on what form that self-determination ought to take. One can, for instance, be in favor of Israel's right to exist, but still ask, What is the most legitimate and democratic form that such an existence ought to take? If one questions the present form, is one therefore anti-Israel? If one holds out for a truly democratic Israel/Palestine, is one therefore anti-Israel? Or is one trying to find a better form for this polity, one that may well involve any number of possibilities: a revised version of Zionism, a post-Zionist Israel, a self-determining Palestine, or an amalgamation of Israel into a greater Israel/Palestine where all race- and religion-based qualifications on rights and entitlements would be eliminated? If one is against a present-day version of Zionism, and offers reasons, reasons that would eliminate all forms of racial discrimination, including all forms of anti-Semitism, then surely one is involved in a critique of Israel that does not immediately qualify as anti-Semitic.

This is not to say that there will not be those who seize upon the fact of critique to further their anti-Semitic aims. That may well take place, and it surely has taken place. I do not mean to dispute this possibility and this reality. But the fact that there are those who will exploit such a critique is not reason enough to silence the critique. If the possibility of that exploitation serves as a reason to quell political dissent, then one has effectively given the domain of public discourse over to those who accept and perpetrate the view that anti-Semitism is authorized by criticisms of Israel, including those who seek to perpetuate anti-Semitism through such criticisms and those who seek to quell such criticisms for fear that they perpetuate anti-Semitism. To remain silent for fear of a possible anti-Semitic appropriation is to keep the very equation of Zionism and Jewishness intact, when it is precisely the separation between the two that guarantees the conditions for critical thinking on this issue. To remain silent for fear of an anti-Semitic appropriation that one deems to be certain is to give up on the possibility of combating anti-Semitism by other means.

What struck me as ironic here is that Summers himself makes the equation of Zionism with Jewishness and, so it seems, of Zionists with Jews, even though this is the very tactic of anti-Semitism. At the same time that this was happening, I found myself on a listserv in which a number of individuals opposed to the current policies of the state of Israel and sometimes opposed to Zionism itself started to engage in this very slippage, sometimes opposing what they called "Zionism" and other times opposing what they called "Jewish" interests. Every time the latter equation took place on the listserv, a number of us objected, and as a consequence several people took themselves off the listserv, unable to bear the slippage any longer. The controversial academic in Manchester, England, Mona Baker, who dismissed two Israeli colleagues from the board of her translation studies journal in an effort to boycott Israeli institutions, offered a weak argument in defense of her act, claiming that there was no way to distinguish between individuals and institutions. In dismissing these individuals, she claimed she was treating them as emblematic of the Israeli state, since they were citizens of that country. But citizens are not the same as states: the very possibility of significant dissent depends upon the difference between them. The presumption of a seamless continuity between Israeli citizens and the Israeli state not only made all Israelis equivalent to state interests, but makes it more difficult for academics outside of Israel to ally with dissidents inside who are taking strong and important stands against the occupation. Mona Baker's conflation of citizens with states was quickly followed, in her own discourse, by a collapse of "Israeli" interests with "Jewish" ones. Her response to the widespread criticism of the act in which she dismissed Israeli scholars from her board was to send around emails on the "academicsforjustice" listserv complaining about "Jewish" newspapers, labeling as "pressure" the opportunity that some such newspapers offered to discuss the issue in print with those she had dismissed. She refused such conversation. At that moment, it seemed, she was not only in a fight against current Israeli policy or, indeed, the structure and basis of legitimation of the Israeli state, but suddenly, now, with "Jews," identified as a lobby that pressures people, a lobby that pressures her. She not only engaged established anti-Semitic stereotypes, but she collapsed the important distinction between Jewishness and Zionism. In her defense, Baker pointed out that one of the Zionist journals enlisting her to participate was called *The Jewish Press*, but the slide from proper name into generic entity remains nevertheless unfortunate. The same criticism that I offered to Summers's view thus applies to Baker as well: it is one thing to oppose Israel in its current form and practices or, indeed, to have critical questions about Zionism itself, but it is quite another to oppose "Jews" or fear from "Jews" or assume that all "Jews" have the same view, that they are all in favor of Israel, identified with Israel or represented by Israel. Oddly, and painfully, it has to be said that at this point, on these occasions Mona Baker and Lawrence Summers make use of a similar premise: Jews are the same as Israel. In the one instance, the premise works in the service of an argument against anti-Semitism; in the second, it works as the effect of anti-Semitism itself. Indeed, it seems to me that one aspect of anti-Semitism or, indeed, of any form of racism is that an entire people is falsely and summarily equated with a given position, view, or disposition. To say that all Jews hold a given view on Israel or are adequately represented by Israel or, conversely, that the acts of Israel, the state, adequately stand for the acts of all Jews, is to conflate Jews with Israel and, therefore, to recirculate an anti-Semitic reduction of Jewishness. Unfortunately, Summers's argument against anti-Semitism makes use of this anti-Semitic premise (which does not mean that he *is* anti-Semitic). We see the anti-Semitism of the premise actively expressed in the remark that Mona Baker makes about the "Jewish" press that is presumptively identified with Israeli state interests (which does not mean that she *is* anti-Semitic).

In holding out for a distinction between Israel and Jews, I am calling for a space of critique and a condition of dissent for Jews who have criticisms of Israel to articulate, but I am also opposing anti-Semitic reductions of Jewishness to Israeli interests. The "Jew" is no more defined by Israel than by anti-Semitic diatribe. The "Jew" exceeds both determinations, and is to be found, substantively, as this diasporic excess, a historically and culturally changing identity that takes no single form and has no single telos. Once the distinction between Israel and Jews is made, an intellectual discussion of both Zionism and anti-Semitism can begin, since it will be as important to understand critically the legacy of Zionism and to debate its future as it will be to track and oppose anti-Semitism as it is promulgated throughout the globe. A progressive Jewish stance will pursue both directions, and will refuse to brand as anti-Semitic the critical impulse or to accept anti-Semitic discourse as a legitimate substitute for critique.

What is needed is a public space in which such issues might be thoughtfully debated, and for academics to support the commitment to academic freedom and intellectual inquiry that would support a thoughtful consideration of these issues. What we are up against here is not only the question of whether certain kinds of ideas and positions can be permitted in public space, but how public space is itself defined by certain kinds of exclusions, certain emerging patterns of censoriousness and censorship. I have considered the way in which the charge of anti-Semitism against those who voice opposition to Israeli policy or to its founding ideology seeks to discredit that point of view as hatred or, indeed, hate speech, and to put into question its permissibility as protected speech or, indeed, valued political commentary. If one cannot voice an objection to violence done by the Israeli state without attracting the charge of anti-Semitism, then the charge works to circumscribe the publicly acceptable domain of speech. It also works to immunize Israeli violence against critique by refusing to countenance the integrity of the claims made against that violence. One is threatened with the label, "anti-Semitic," in the same way that within the US, to oppose the most recent US wars earns one the label of "traitor," or "terrorist sympathizer" or, indeed, "treasonous." These are threats with profound psychological consequence. They seek to control political behavior by imposing unbearable, stigmatized modes of identification which most people will want more than anything to avoid identification with. Fearing the identification, they fail to speak out. But such threats of stigmatization can and must be weathered, and this can only be done with the support of other actors, others who speak with you, and against the threat that seeks to silence political speech. The threat of being called "anti-Semitic" seeks to control, at the level of the subject, what one is willing to say out loud and, at the level of society in general, to circumscribe what can and cannot be permissibly spoken out loud in the public sphere. More dramatically, these are threats that *decide* the defining limits of the public sphere through setting limits on the speakable. The world of public discourse, in other words, will be that space and time from which those critical perspectives will be excluded. The exclusion of those criticisms will effectively establish the boundaries of the public itself, and the public will come to understand itself as one that does not speak out, critically, in the face of obvious and illegitimate violence—unless, of course, a certain collective courage takes hold.

5

PRECARIOUS LIFE

... the surplus of every sociality over every solitude.

Levinas

At a recent meeting, I listened to a university press director tell a story. It was unclear whether he identified with the point of view from which the story was told, or whether he was relaying the bad news reluctantly. But the story he told was about another meeting, where he was listening, and there a president of a university made the point that no one is reading humanities books anymore, that the humanities have nothing more to offer or, rather, nothing to offer for our times. I'm not sure whether he was saying that the university president was saying that the humanities had lost their moral authority, but it sounded like this was, in fact, someone's view, and that it was a view to take seriously. There was an ensuing set of discussions at the same meeting in which it was not always possible to tell which view was owned by whom, or whether anyone really was willing to own a view. It was a discussion that turned on the question, Have the humanities undermined themselves, with all their relativism and questioning and "critique," or have the humanities been undermined by all those who *oppose* all that relativism and questioning and "critique"? Someone has undermined the humanities, or some group of people has, but it was unclear who, and it was unclear who thought this was true. I started to wonder whether I was not in the middle of the humanities quandary itself, the one in which no one knows who is speaking and in what voice, and with what intent. Does anyone stand by the words they utter? Can we still trace those words to a speaker or, indeed, a writer? And which message, exactly, was being sent?

Of course, it would be paradoxical if I were now to argue that what we really need is to tether discourse to authors, and in that way we will reestablish both authors and authority. I did my own bit of work, along with many of you, in trying to cut that tether. But what I do think is missing, and what I would like to see and hear return is a consideration of the structure of address itself. Because although I did not know in whose voice this person was speaking, whether the voice was his own or not, I did feel that I was being addressed, and that something called the humanities was being derided from some direction or another. To respond to this address seems an important obligation during these times. This obligation is something other than the rehabilitation of the author–subject *per se*. It is about a mode of response that follows upon having been addressed, a comportment toward the Other only after the Other has made a demand upon me, accused me of a failing, or asked me to assume a responsibility. This is an exchange that cannot be assimilated into the schema in which the subject is over here as a topic to be reflexively interrogated, and the Other is over there, as a theme to be purveyed. The structure of address is important for understanding how moral authority is introduced and sustained if we accept not just that we address others when we speak, but that in some way we come to exist, as it were, in the moment of being addressed, and something about our existence proves precarious when that address fails. More emphatically, however, what binds us morally has to do with how we are addressed by others in ways that we cannot avert or avoid; this impingement by the other's address constitutes us first and foremost against our will or, perhaps put more appropriately, prior to the formation of our will. So if we think that moral authority is about finding one's will and standing by it, stamping one's name upon one's will, it may be that we miss the very mode by which moral demands are relayed. That is, we miss the situation of being addressed, the demand that comes from elsewhere, sometimes a nameless elsewhere, by which our obligations are articulated and pressed upon us.

Indeed, this conception of what is morally binding is not one that I give myself; it does not proceed from my autonomy or my reflexivity. It comes to me from elsewhere, unbidden, unexpected, and unplanned. In fact, it tends to ruin my plans, and if my plans are ruined, that may well be the sign that something is morally binding upon me. We think of presidents as wielding speech acts in willful ways, so when the director of a university press, or the president of a university speaks, we expect to know what they are saying, and to whom they are speaking, and with what intent. We expect the address to be authoritative and, in that sense, to be binding. But presidential speech is strange these days, and it would take a better rhetorician than I am to understand the mysteriousness of its ways. Why should it be, for instance, that Iraq is called a threat to the security of the "civilized world" while missiles flying from North Korea, and even the attempted hostage-taking of US boats, are called "regional issues"? And if the US President was urged by the majority of the world to withdraw his threat of war, why does he not seem to feel obligated by this address? But given the shambles into which presidential address has fallen, perhaps we should think more seriously about the relation between modes of address and moral authority. This may help us to know what values the humanities have to offer, and what the situation of discourse is in which moral authority becomes binding.

I would like to consider the "face," the notion introduced by Emmanuel Levinas, to explain how it is that others make moral claims upon us, address moral demands to us, ones that we do not ask for, ones that we are not free to refuse. Levinas makes a preliminary demand upon me, but his is not the only demand that I am bound to follow these days. I will trace what seem to me the outlines of a possible Jewish ethic of non-violence. Then I will relate this to some of the more pressing questions of violence and ethics that are upon us now. The Levinasian notion of the "face" has caused critical consternation for a long time. It seems to be that the "face" of what he calls the "Other" makes an ethical demand upon me, and yet we do not know which demand it makes. The "face" of the other cannot be read for a secret meaning, and the imperative it delivers is not immediately translatable into a prescription that might be linguistically formulated and followed.

Levinas writes:

The approach to the face is the most basic mode of responsibility .... The face is not in front of me (*en face de moi*), but above me; it is the other before death, looking through and exposing death. Secondly, the face is the other who asks me not to let him die alone, as if to do so were to become an accomplice in his death. Thus the face says to me: you shall not kill. In the relation to the face I am exposed as a usurper of the place of the other. The celebrated "right to existence" that Spinoza called the *conatus essendi* and defined as the basic principle of all intelligibility is challenged by the relation to the face. Accordingly, my duty to respond to the other suspends my natural right to self-survival, *le droit vitale*. My ethical relation of love for the other stems from the fact that the self cannot survive by itself alone, cannot find meaning within its own being-in-the-world .... To expose myself to the vulnerability of the face is to put my ontological right to existence into question. In ethics, the other's right to exist has primacy over my own, a primacy epitomized in the ethical edict: you shall not kill, you shall not jeopardize the life of the other.[1]

Levinas writes further:

The face is what one cannot kill, or at least it is that whose meaning consists in saying, "thou shalt not kill." Murder, it is true, is a banal fact: one can kill the Other; the ethical exigency is not an ontological necessity .... It also appears in the Scriptures, to which the humanity of man is exposed inasmuch as it is engaged in the world. But to speak truly, the appearance in being of these "ethical peculiarities" —the humanity of man—is a rupture of being. It is significant, even if being resumes and recovers itself.[2]

So the face, strictly speaking, does not speak, but what the face means is nevertheless conveyed by the commandment, "Thou shalt not kill." It conveys this commandment without precisely speaking it. It would seem that we can use this biblical command to understand something of the face's meaning, but something is missing here, since the "face" does not speak in the sense that the mouth does; the face is neither reducible to the mouth nor, indeed, to anything the mouth has to utter. Someone or something else speaks when the face is likened to a certain kind of speech; it is a speech that does not come from a mouth or, if it does, has no ultimate origin or meaning there. In fact, in an essay entitled "Peace and Proximity," Levinas makes plain that "the face is not exclusively a human face."[3] To explain this, he refers to Vassili Grossman's text *Life and Fate*, which he describes as:

> the story ... of the families, wives, and parents of political detainees traveling to the Lubyanka in Moscow for the latest news. A line is formed at the counter, a line where one can see only the backs of others. A woman awaits her turn: [She] had never thought that the human back could be so expressive, and could convey states of mind in such a penetrating way. Persons approaching the counter had a particular way of craning their neck and their back, their raised shoulders with shoulder blades like springs, which seemed to cry, sob, and scream. (PP, 167)

Here the term "face" operates as a catachresis: "face" describes the human back, the craning of the neck, the raising of the shoulder blades like "springs." And these bodily parts, in turn, are said to cry and to sob and to scream, as if they were a face or, rather, a face with a mouth, a throat, or indeed, just a mouth and throat from which vocalizations emerge that do not settle into words. The face is to be found in the back and the neck, but it is not quite a face. The sounds that come from or through the face are agonized, suffering. So we can see already that the "face" seems to consist in a series of displacements such that a face is figured as a back which, in turn, is figured as a scene of agonized vocalization. And though there are many names strung in a row here, they end with a figure for what cannot be named, an utterance that is not, strictly speaking, linguistic. Thus the face, the name for the face, and the words by which we are to understand its meaning—"Thou shalt not kill"—do not quite deliver the meaning of the face, since at the end of the line, it seems, it is precisely the wordless vocalization of suffering that marks the limits of linguistic translation here. The face, if we are to put words to its meaning, will be that for which no words really work; the face seems to be a kind of sound, the sound of language evacuating its sense, the sonorous substratum of vocalization that precedes and limits the delivery of any semantic sense.

At the end of this description, Levinas appends the following lines, which do not quite accomplish the sentence form: "The face as the extreme precariousness of the other. Peace as awakeness to the precariousness of the other" (PP, 167). Both statements are similes, and they both avoid the verb, especially the copula. They do not say that the face *is* that precariousness, or that peace *is* the mode of being awake to an Other's precariousness. Both phrases are substitutions that refuse any commitment to the order of being. Levinas tells us, in fact, that "humanity is a rupture of being" and in the previous remarks he performs that suspension and rupture in an utterance that is both less and more than a sentence form. To respond to the face, to understand its meaning, means to be awake to what is precarious in another life or, rather, the precariousness of life itself. This cannot be an awakeness, to use his word, to my own life, and then an extrapolation from an understanding of my own precariousness to an understanding of another's precarious life. It has to be an understanding of the precariousness of the Other. This is what makes the face belong to the sphere of ethics. Levinas writes, "the face of the other in its precariousness and defenselessness, is for me at once the temptation to kill and the call to peace, the 'You shall not kill'" (*PP*, 167). This last remark suggests something quite disarming in several senses. Why would it be that the very precariousness of the Other would produce for me a temptation to kill? Or why would it produce the temptation to kill *at the same time* that it delivers a demand for peace? Is there something about my apprehension of the Other's precariousness that makes me want to kill the Other? Is it the simple vulnerability of the Other that becomes a murderous temptation for me? If the Other, the Other's face, which after all carries the meaning of this precariousness, at once tempts me with murder and prohibits me from acting upon it, then the face operates to produce a struggle for me, and establishes this struggle at the heart of ethics. It would seem that it is God's voice that is represented by the human voice, since it is God who says, through Moses, "Thou shalt not kill." The face that at once makes me murderous and prohibits me from murder is the one that speaks in a voice that is not its own, speaks in a voice that is no human voice.[4] So the face makes various utterances at once: it bespeaks an agony, an injurability, at the same time that it bespeaks a divine prohibition against killing.[5]

Earlier in "Peace and Proximity," Levinas considers the vocation of Europe, and wonders whether the "Thou shalt not kill" is not precisely what one should hear in the very meaning of European culture. It is unclear where his Europe begins or ends, whether it has geographical boundaries, or whether it is produced every time the commandment is spoken or conveyed. This is, already, a curious Europe whose meaning is conjectured to consist in the words of the Hebrew God, whose civilizational status, as it were, depends upon the transmission of divine interdictions from the Bible. It is Europe in which Hebraism has taken the place of Hellenism, and Islam remains unspeakable. Perhaps Levinas is telling us that the only Europe that ought to be called Europe is the one that elevates the Old Testament over civil and secular law. In any case, he seems to be returning to the primacy of interdiction to the meaning of civilization itself. And though we might be tempted to understand this as a nefarious Eurocentrism, it is probably also important to see that there is no recognizable Europe that can be derived from his view. In fact, it is not the existence of the interdiction against murder that makes Europe Europe, but the anxiety and the desire that the interdiction produces. As he continues to explain how this commandment works, he refers to Genesis, chapter 32, in which Jacob learns of his brother and rival Esau's imminent approach. Levinas writes, "Jacob is troubled by the news that his brother Esau—friend or foe—is marching to meet him 'at the head of four hundred men.' Verse 8 tells us: 'Jacob was greatly afraid and anxious.'" Levinas then turns to the commentator Rashi to understand "the difference between fright and anxiety," and concludes that "[Jacob] was frightened of his own death but was anxious he might have to kill" (PP, 164).

Of course, it is unclear still why Levinas would assume that one of the first or primary responses to another's precariousness is the desire to kill. Why would it be that the spring of the shoulder blades, the craning of the neck, the agonized vocalization conveying another's suffering would prompt in anyone a lust for violence? It must be that Esau over there, with his four hundred men, threatens to kill me, or looks like he will, and that in relation to that menacing Other or, indeed, the one whose face represents a menace, I must defend myself to preserve my life. Levinas explains, though, that murdering in the name of self-preservation is not justified, that self-preservation is never a sufficient condition for the ethical justification of violence. This seems, then, like an extreme pacifism, an absolute pacifism, and it may well be. We may or may not want to accept these consequences, but we should consider the dilemma they pose as constitutive of the ethical anxiety: "Frightened for his own life, but anxious he might have to kill." There is fear for one's own survival, and there is anxiety about hurting the Other, and these two impulses are at war with each other, like siblings fighting. But they are at war with each other in order *not* to be at war, and this seems to be the point. For the non-violence that Levinas seems to promote does not come from a peaceful place, but rather from a constant tension between the fear of undergoing violence and the fear of inflicting violence. I could put an end to my fear of my own death by obliterating the other, although I would have to keep obliterating, especially if there are four hundred men behind him, and they all have families and friends, if not a nation or two behind them. I could put an end to my anxiety about becoming a murderer by reconciling myself to the ethical justification for inflicting violence and death under such conditions. I could bring out the utilitarian calculus, or appeal to the intrinsic rights of individuals to protect and preserve their own rights. We can imagine uses of both consequentialist and deontological justifications that would give me many opportunities to inflict violence righteously. A consequentialist might argue that it would be for the good of the many. A deontologist might appeal to the intrinsic worth of my own life. They could also be used to dispute the primacy of the interdiction on murder, an interdiction in the face of which I would continue to feel my anxiety.

Although Levinas counsels that self-preservation is not a good enough reason to kill, he also presumes that the desire to kill is primary to human beings. If the first impulse towards the other's vulnerability is the desire to kill, the ethical injunction is precisely to militate against that first impulse. In psychoanalytic terms, that would mean marshaling the desire to kill in the service of an internal desire to kill one's own aggression and sense of priority. The result would probably be neurotic, but it may be that psychoanalysis meets a limit here. For Levinas, it is the ethical itself that gets one out of the circuitry of bad conscience, the logic by which the prohibition against aggression becomes the internal conduit for aggression itself. Aggression is then turned back upon oneself in the form of super-egoic cruelty. If the ethical moves us beyond bad conscience, it is because bad conscience is, after all, only a negative version of narcissism, and so still a form of narcissism. The face of the Other comes to me from outside, and interrupts that narcissistic circuit. The face of the Other calls me out of narcissism towards something finally more important.

Levinas writes:

> The Other is the sole being I can wish to kill. I can wish. And yet this power is quite the contrary of power. The triumph of this power is its defeat as power. At the very moment when my power to kill realizes itself, the other has escaped me .... I have not looked at him in the face, I have not encountered his face. The temptation of total negation ... this is the presence of the face. To be in relation with the other face to face is to be unable to kill. It is also the situation of discourse. (9)

It is also the situation of discourse ...

... this last is no idle claim. Levinas explains in one interview that "face and discourse are tied. It speaks, it is in this that it renders possible and begins all discourse" (*EI*, 87). Since what the face "says" is "Thou shalt not kill," it would appear that it is through this primary commandment that speaking first comes into being, so that speaking first comes into being against the backdrop of this possible murder. More generally, discourse makes an ethical claim upon us precisely because, prior to speaking, something is spoken to us. In a simple sense, and perhaps not quite as Levinas intended, we are first spoken to, addressed, by an Other, before we assume language for ourselves. And we can conclude further that it is only on the condition that we are addressed that we are able to make use of language. It is in this sense that the Other is the condition of discourse. If the Other is obliterated, so too is language, since language cannot survive outside of the conditions of address.

But let us remember that Levinas has also told us that the face—which is the face of the Other, and so the ethical demand made by the Other—is that vocalization of agony that is not yet language or no longer language, the one by which we are wakened to the precariousness of the Other's life, the one that rouses at once the temptation to murder and the interdiction against it. Why would it be that the inability to kill is the situation of discourse? Is it rather that the tension between fear for one's own life and anxiety about becoming a murderer constitutes the ambivalence that is the situation of discourse? That situation is one in which we are addressed, in which the Other directs language towards us. That language communicates the precariousness of life that establishes the ongoing tension of a non-violent ethics. The situation of discourse is not the same as what is said or, indeed, what is sayable. For Levinas, the situation of discourse consists in the fact that language arrives as an address we do not will, and by which we are, in an original sense, captured, if not, in Levinas's terms, held hostage. So there is a certain violence already in being addressed, given a name, subject to a set of impositions, compelled to respond to an exacting alterity. No one controls the terms by which one is addressed, at least not in the most fundamental way. To be addressed is to be, from the start, deprived of will, and to have that deprivation exist as the basis of one's situation in discourse.

Within the ethical frame of the Levinasian position, we begin by positing a dyad. But the sphere of politics, in his terms, is one in which there are always more than two subjects at play in the scene. Indeed, I may decide *not* to invoke my own desire to preserve my life as a justification for violence, but what if violence is done to someone I love? What if there is an Other who does violence to another Other?

To which Other do I respond ethically? Which Other do I put before myself? Or do I then stand by? Derrida claims that to try and respond to every Other can only result in a situation of radical irresponsibility. And the Spinozists, the Nietzscheans, the utilitarians, and the Freudians all ask, "Can I invoke the imperative to preserve the life *of the Other* even if I cannot invoke this right of self-preservation for myself?" And is it really possible to sidestep self-preservation in the way that Levinas implies? Spinoza writes in *The Ethics* that the desire to live the right life requires the desire to live, to persist in one's own being, suggesting that ethics must always marshal some life drives, even if, as a super-egoic state, ethics threatens to become a pure culture of the death drive. It is possible, even easy, to read Levinas as an elevated masochist and it does not help us to avert that conclusion when we consider that, when asked what he thought of psycho-analysis, he is said to have responded, *is that not a form of pornography?*

But the reason to consider Levinas in the context of today is at least twofold. First, he gives us a way of thinking about the relationship between representation and humanization, a relationship that is not as straightforward as we might like to think. If critical thinking has something to say about or to the present situation, it may well be in the domain of representation where humanization and dehumanization occur ceaselessly. Second, he offers, within a tradition of Jewish philosophy, an account of the relationship between violence and ethics that has some important implications for thinking through what an ethic of Jewish non-violence might be. This strikes me as a timely and urgent question for many of us, especially those of us supporting the emergent moment of post-Zionism within Judaism. For now, I would like to reconsider first the problematic of humanization if we approach it through the figure of the face.

When we consider the ordinary ways that we think about humanization and dehumanization, we find the assumption that those who
gain representation, especially self-representation, have a better chance
of being humanized, and those who have no chance to represent
themselves run a greater risk of being treated as less than human,
regarded as less than human, or indeed, not regarded at all. We have
a paradox before us because Levinas has made clear that the face is not
exclusively a human face, and yet it is a condition for humanization.[6]
On the other hand, there is the use of the face, within the media, in
order to effect a dehumanization. It would seem that personification
does not always humanize. For Levinas, it may well evacuate the face
that does humanize; and I hope to show, personification sometimes
performs its own dehumanization. How do we come to know the
difference between the inhuman but humanizing face, for Levinas,
and the dehumanization that can also take place through the face?

We may have to think of different ways that violence can happen:
one is precisely *through* the production of the face, the face of Osama
bin Laden, the face of Yasser Arafat, the face of Saddam Hussein.
What has been done with these faces in the media? They are framed,
surely, but they are also playing to the frame. And the result is
invariably tendentious. These are media portraits that are often mar-
shaled in the service of war, as if bin Laden's face were the face of
terror itself, as if Arafat were the face of deception, as if Hussein's face
were the face of contemporary tyranny. And then there is the face of
Colin Powell, as it is framed and circulated, seated before the shrouded
canvas of Picasso's *Guernica*: a face that is foregrounded, we might say,
against a background of effacement. Then there are the faces of the
Afghan girls who stripped off, or let fall, their burkas. One week last
winter, I visited a political theorist who proudly displayed these faces
on his refrigerator door, right next to some apparently valuable super-
market coupons, as a sign of the success of democracy. A few days

later, I attended a conference in which I heard a talk about the important cultural meanings of the burka, the way in which it signifies belonging-ness to a community and religion, a family, an extended history of kin relations, an exercise of modesty and pride, a protection against shame, and operates as well as a veil behind which, and through which, feminine agency can and does work.[7] The fear of the speaker was that the destruction of the burka, as if it were a sign of repression, backwardness or, indeed, a resistance to cultural modernity itself, would result in a significant decimation of Islamic culture and the extension of US cultural assumptions about how sexuality and agency ought to be organized and represented. According to the triumphalist photos that dominated the front page of the *New York Times*, these young women bared their faces as an act of liberation, an act of gratitude to the US military, and an expression of a pleasure that had become suddenly and ecstatically permissible. The American viewer was ready, as it were, to see the face, and it was to the camera, and for the camera, after all, that the face was finally bared, where it became, in a flash, a symbol of successfully exported American cultural progress. It became bared to us, at that moment, and we were, as it were, in possession of the face; not only did our cameras capture it, but we arranged for the face to capture our triumph, and act as the rationale for our violence, the incursion on sovereignty, the deaths of civilians. Where is loss in that face? And where is the suffering over war? Indeed, the photographed face seemed to conceal or displace the face in the Levinasian sense, since we saw and heard through that face no vocalization of grief or agony, no sense of the precariousness of life.

So we seem to be charting a certain ambivalence. In a strange way, all of these faces humanize the events of the last year or so; they give a human face to Afghan women; they give a face to terror; they give a face to evil. But is the face humanizing in each and every instance? And if it is humanizing in some instances, in what form does this humanization occur, and is there also a dehumanization performed in and through the face? Do we encounter those faces in the Levinasian sense, or are these, in various ways, images that, through their frame, produce the paradigmatically human, become the very cultural means through which the paradigmatically human is established? Although it is tempting to think that the images themselves establish the visual norm for the human, one that ought to be emulated or embodied, this would be a mistake, since in the case of bin Laden or Saddam Hussein the paradigmatically human is understood to reside outside the frame; this is the human face in its deformity and extremity, not the one with which you are asked to identify. Indeed, the disidentification is incited through the hyperbolic absorption of evil into the face itself, the eyes. And if we are to understand ourselves as interpellated anywhere in these images, it is precisely as the unrepresented viewer, the one who looks on, the one who is captured by no image at all, but whose charge it is to capture and subdue, if not eviscerate, the image at hand. Similarly, although we might want to champion the suddenly bared faces of the young Afghan women as the celebration of the human, we have to ask in what narrative function these images are mobilized, whether the incursion into Afghanistan was really in the name of feminism, and in what form of feminism did it belatedly clothe itself. Most importantly, though, it seems we have to ask what scenes of pain and grief these images cover over and derealize. Indeed, all of these images seem to suspend the precariousness of life; they either represent American triumph, or provide an incitement for American military triumph in the future. *They are the spoils of war or they are the targets of war*. And in this sense, we might say that the face is, in every instance, defaced, and that this is one of the representational and philosophical consequences of war itself.

It is important to distinguish among kinds of unrepresentability. In the first instance, there is the Levinasian view according to which there is a "face" which no face can fully exhaust, the face understood as human suffering, as the cry of human suffering, which can take no direct representation. Here the "face" is always a figure for something that is not literally a face. Other human expressions, however, seem to be figurable as a "face" even though they are not faces, but sounds or emissions of another order. The cry that is represented through the figure of the face is one that confounds the senses and produces a clearly improper comparison: that cannot be right, for the face is not a sound. And yet, the face can stand for the sound precisely because it is *not* the sound. In this sense, the figure underscores the incommensurability of the face with whatever it represents. Strictly speaking, then, the face does not represent anything, in the sense that it fails to capture and deliver that to which it refers.

For Levinas, then, the human is not *represented by* the face. Rather, the human is indirectly affirmed in that very disjunction that makes representation impossible, and this disjunction is conveyed in the impossible representation. For representation to convey the human, then, representation must not only fail, but it must *show* its failure. There is something unrepresentable that we nevertheless seek to represent, and that paradox must be retained in the representation we give.

In this sense, the human is not identified with what is represented but neither is it identified with the unrepresentable; it is, rather, that which limits the success of any representational practice. The face is not "effaced" in this failure of representation, but is constituted in that very possibility. Something altogether different happens, however, when the face operates in the service of a personification that claims to "capture" the human being in question. For Levinas, the human cannot be captured through the representation, and we can see that some loss of the human takes place when it is "captured" by the image.[8]

An example of that kind of "capture" takes place when evil is personified through the face. A certain commensurability is asserted between that ostensible evil and the face. This face *is* evil, and the evil that the face *is* extends to the evil that belongs to humans in general—generalized evil. We personify the evil or military triumph through a face that is supposed to be, to capture, to contain the very idea for which it stands. In this case, we cannot hear the face through the face. The face here masks the sounds of human suffering and the proximity we might have to the precariousness of life itself.

The face over there, though, the one whose meaning is portrayed as captured by evil is precisely the one that is not human, not in the Levinasian sense. The "I" who sees that face is not identified with it: the face represents that for which no identification is possible, an accomplishment of dehumanization and a condition for violence.

Of course, a fuller elaboration of this topic would have to parse the various ways that representation works in relation to humanization and dehumanization. Sometimes there are triumphalist images that give us the idea of the human with whom we are to identify, for instance the patriotic hero who expands our own ego boundary ecstatically into that of the nation. No understanding of the relationship between the image and humanization can take place without a consideration of the conditions and meanings of identification and disidentification. It is worth noting, however, that identification always relies upon a difference that it seeks to overcome, and that its aim is accomplished only by reintroducing the difference it claims to have vanquished. The one with whom I identify is not me, and that "not being me" is the condition of the identification. Otherwise, as

Jacqueline Rose reminds us, identification collapses into identity, which spells the death of identification itself.[9] This difference internal to identification is crucial, and, in a way, it shows us that dis-identification is part of the common practice of identification itself. The triumphalist image can communicate an impossible overcoming of this difference, a kind of identification that believes that it has overcome the difference that is the condition of its own possibility. The critical image, if we can speak that way, works this difference in the same way as the Levinasian image; it must not only fail to capture its referent, but *show* this failing.

The demand for a truer image, for more images, for images that convey the full horror and reality of the suffering has its place and importance. The erasure of that suffering through the prohibition of images and representations more generally circumscribes the sphere of appearance, what we can see and what we can know. But it would be a mistake to think that we only need to find the right and true images, and that a certain reality will then be conveyed. The reality is not conveyed by what is represented within the image, but through the challenge to representation that reality delivers.[10]

The media's evacuation of the human through the image has to be understood, though, in terms of the broader problem that normative schemes of intelligibility establish what will and will not be human, what will be a livable life, what will be a grievable death. These normative schemes operate not only by producing ideals of the human that differentiate among those who are more and less human. Sometimes they produce images of the less than human, in the guise of the human, to show how the less than human disguises itself, and threatens to deceive those of us who might think we recognize another human there, in that face. But sometimes these normative schemes work precisely through providing no image, no name, no narrative, so that there never was a life, and there never was a death.

These are two distinct forms of normative power: one operates through producing a symbolic identification of the face with the inhuman, foreclosing our apprehension of the human in the scene; the other works through radical effacement, so that there never was a human, there never was a life, and no murder has, therefore, ever taken place. In the first instance, something that has already emerged into the realm of appearance needs to be disputed as recognizably human; in the second instance, the public realm of appearance is itself constituted on the basis of the exclusion of that image. The task at hand is to establish modes of public seeing and hearing that might well respond to the cry of the human within the sphere of appearance, a sphere in which the trace of the cry has become hyperbolically inflated to rationalize a gluttonous nationalism, or fully obliterated, where both alternatives turn out to be the same. We might consider this as one of the philosophical and representational implications of war, because politics—and power—work in part through regulating what can appear, what can be heard.

Of course, these schemas of intelligibility are tacitly and forcefully mandated by those corporations that monopolize control over the mainstream media with strong interests in maintaining US military power. The war coverage has brought into relief the need for a broad de-monopolozing of media interests, legislation for which has been, predictably, highly contested on Capitol Hill. We think of these interests as controlling rights of ownership, but they are also, simultaneously, deciding what will and will not be publicly recognizable as reality. They do not show violence, but there is a violence in the frame in what is shown. That latter violence is the mechanism through which certain lives and deaths either remain unrepresentable or become represented in ways that effects their capture (once again) by the war effort. The first is an effacement through occlusion; the second is an effacement through representation itself.

What is the relation between the violence by which these ungrievable lives were lost and the prohibition on their public grievability? Is
the prohibition on grieving the continuation of the violence itself?
And does the prohibition on grieving demand a tight control on the
reproduction of images and words? How does the prohibition on
grieving emerge as a circumscription of representability, so that our
national melancholia becomes tightly fitted into the frame for what
can be said, what can be shown? Is this not the site where we can
read, if we still read, the way that melancholia becomes inscribed
as the limits of what can be thought? The derealization of loss—the
insensitivity to human suffering and death—becomes the mechanism
through which dehumanization is accomplished. This derealization
takes place neither inside nor outside the image, but through the very
framing by which the image is contained.

In the initial campaign of the war against Iraq, the US government advertised its military feats as an overwhelming visual
phenomenon. That the US government and military called this a
"shock and awe" strategy suggests that they were producing a visual
spectacle that numbs the senses and, like the sublime itself, puts out
of play the very capacity to think. This production takes place not
only for the Iraqi population on the ground, whose senses are
supposed to be done in by this spectacle, but also for the consumers
of war who rely on CNN or Fox, the network that regularly inter-
spersed its war coverage on television with the claim that it is the
"most trustworthy" news source on the war. The "shock and awe"
strategy seeks not only to produce an aesthetic dimension to war, but
to exploit and instrumentalize the visual aesthetics as part of a war
strategy itself. CNN has provided much of these visual aesthetics.
And although the *New York Times* belatedly came out against the war,
it also adorned its front pages on a daily basis with romantic images
of military ordnance against the setting sun in Iraq or "bombs

bursting in air" above the streets and homes of Baghdad (which are not surprisingly occluded from view). Of course, it was the spectacular destruction of the World Trade Center that first made a claim upon the "shock and awe" effect, and the US recently displayed for all the world to see that it can and will be equally destructive. The media becomes entranced by the sublimity of destruction, and voices of dissent and opposition must find a way to intervene upon this desensitizing dream machine in which the massive destruction of lives and homes, sources of water, electricity, and heat, are produced as a delirious sign of a resuscitated US military power.

Indeed, the graphic photos of US soldiers dead and decapitated in Iraq, and then the photos of children maimed and killed by US bombs, were both refused by the mainstream media, supplanted with footage that always took the aerial view, an aerial view whose perspective is established and maintained by state power. And yet, the moment the bodies executed by the Hussein regime were uncovered, they made it to the front page of the *New York Times*, since those bodies must be grieved. The outrage over their deaths motivates the war effort, as it moves on to its managerial phase, which differs very little from what is commonly called "an occupation."

Tragically, it seems that the US seeks to preempt violence against itself by waging violence first, but the violence it fears is the violence it engenders. I do not mean to suggest by this that the US is responsible in some causal way for the attacks on its citizens. And I do not exonerate Palestinian suicide bombers, regardless of the terrible conditions that animate their murderous acts. There is, however, some distance to be traveled between living in terrible conditions, suffering serious, even unbearable injuries, and resolving on murderous acts. President Bush traveled that distance quickly, calling for "an end to grief" after a mere ten days of flamboyant mourning. Suffering can yield an experience of humility, of vulnerability, of impressionability and dependence, and these can become resources, if we do not "resolve" them too quickly; they can move us beyond and against the vocation of the paranoid victim who regenerates infinitely the justifications for war. It is as much a matter of wrestling ethically with one's own murderous impulses, impulses that seek to quell an overwhelming fear, as it is a matter of apprehending the suffering of others and taking stock of the suffering one has inflicted.

In the Vietnam War, it was the pictures of the children burning and dying from napalm that brought the US public to a sense of shock, outrage, remorse, and grief. These were precisely pictures we were not supposed to see, and they disrupted the visual field and the entire sense of public identity that was built upon that field. The images furnished a reality, but they also showed a reality that disrupted the hegemonic field of representation itself. Despite their graphic effectivity, the images pointed somewhere else, beyond themselves, to a life and to a precariousness that they could not show. It was from that apprehension of the precariousness of those lives we destroyed that many US citizens came to develop an important and vital consensus against the war. But if we continue to discount the words that deliver that message to us, and if the media will not run those pictures, and if those lives remain unnameable and ungrievable, if they do not appear in their precariousness and their destruction, we will not be moved. We will not return to a sense of ethical outrage that is, distinctively, for an Other, in the name of an Other. We cannot, under contemporary conditions of representation, hear the agonized cry or be compelled or commanded by the face. We have been turned away from the face, sometimes through the very image of the face, one that is meant to convey the inhuman, the already dead, that which is not precariousness and cannot, therefore, be killed; this is the face that we are nevertheless asked to kill, as if ridding the world of this face would return us to the human rather than consummate our own inhumanity. One would need to hear the face as it speaks in something other than language to know the precariousness of life that is at stake. But what media will let us know and feel that frailty, know and feel at the limits of representation as it is currently cultivated and maintained? If the humanities has a future as cultural criticism, and cultural criticism has a task at the present moment, it is no doubt to return us to the human where we do not expect to find it, in its frailty and at the limits of its capacity to make sense. We would have to interrogate the emergence and vanishing of the human at the limits of what we can know, what we can hear, what we can see, what we can sense. This might prompt us, affectively, to reinvigorate the intellectual projects of critique, of questioning, of coming to understand the difficulties and demands of cultural translation and dissent, and to create a sense of the public in which oppositional voices are not feared, degraded or dismissed, but valued for the instigation to a sensate democracy they occasionally perform.

NOTES

1 EXPLANATION AND EXONERATION, OR WHAT WE CAN HEAR

1. *Guardian*, September 29, 2001.
2. Mary Kaldor, *The Nation*, November 5, 2001, p. 16.
3. Forbes.com, October 11, 2001.
4. *New York Times*, November 2, 2001.

2 VIOLENCE, MOURNING, POLITICS

1. Sigmund Freud, *Mourning and Melancholia* (1917) Standard Edition, 14: pp. 243–58, London: Hogarth Press, 1957.
2. Sigmund Freud, *The Ego and the Id* (1923) Standard Edition, 19: pp. 12–66, London: Hogarth Press, 1961.

3. Sigmund Freud, *Mourning and Melancholia*.
4. Ibid.
5. William Safire, "All Is Not Changed", *New York Times*, September 27, 2001, p. A:21.
6. "A Nation Challenged; President Bush's Address on Terrorism before a Joint Meeting of Congress," *New York Times*, September 21, 2001, p. B:4.
7. Richard Garfield, "Morbidity and Mortality among Iraqi Children from 1990 through 1998: Assessing the Impact of the Gulf War and Economic Sanctions," in *Fourth Freedom Forum*, March, 2002. See www.fourthfreedom.org/php/p-index.php?hinc=garf.hinc.
8. The memorials read as follows: "In loving memory of Kamla Abu Sa'id, 42, and her daughter, Amna Abu-Sa'id, 13, both Palestinians from the El Bureij refugee camps. Kamla and her daughter were killed May 26, 2002 by Israeli troops, while working on a farm in the Gaza Strip. In loving memory of Ahmed Abu Seer, 7, a Palestinian child, he was killed in his home with bullets. Ahmed died of fatal shrapnel wounds to his heart and lung. Ahmed was a second-grader at Al-Sidaak elementary school in Nablus, he will be missed by all who knew him. In loving memory of Fatime Ibrahim Zakarna, 30, and her two children, Bassem, 4, and Suhair, 3 all Palestinian. Mother and children were killed May 6, 2002 by Israeli soldiers while picking grape leaves in a field in the Kabatiya village. They leave behind Mohammed Yussef Zukarneh, husband and father, and Yasmine, daughter and age 6." These memorials were submitted by the San Francisco chapter of Arab-American Christians for Peace. The *Chronicle* refused to run the memorials, even though these deaths were covered by, and verified by, the Israeli Press (private email).
9. Daniel Pearl's wife Marianne's statement in Felicity Barringer and Douglas Jehl, "US Says Video Shows Captors Killed Reporter," *New York Times*, February 22, 2002, p. A:1.

10. Gayatri Chakravorti Spivak, *A Critique of Postcolonial Reason: Toward a History of the Vanishing Present*, Cambridge, Mass.: Harvard University Press, 1999, p. 303.

11. See Judith Butler, *Antigone's Claim: Kinship Between Life and Death*, New York: Columbia University Press, 2000.

12. Joan W. Scott, "Feminist Reverberations," unpublished paper presented at Twelfth Berkshire Conference on the History of Women, June 2002, University of Connecticut at Storrs.

13. Chandra Mohanty, "Under Western Eyes: Feminist Scholarship and Colonial Discourses," in *Third World Women and the Politics of Feminism*, ed. Chandra Mohanty, Ann Russo and Lourdes Torres, Indianapolis: Indiana University Press, 1991, pp. 61–88.

14. See also Lila Abu-Lughod, "Do Muslim Women Really Need Saving?" paper presented at symposium "Responding to War," Columbia University, February 1, 2002; and "Interview with Nermeen Shaikh," *Asia Source*, March 20, 2002, http://www. asiasource.org/news/special_reports/lila.cfm. Lila Abu-Lughod, ed., *Remaking Women: Feminism and Modernity in the Middle East*, Princeton, NJ: Princeton University Press, 1998.

15. Mahasweta Devi, *Imaginary Maps: Three Stories*, trans. and intro. Gayatri Chakravorty Spivak, New York and London: Routledge, 1995, p. 199.

16. Adriana Cavarero, *Relating Narratives: Storytelling and Selfhood*, trans. P. Kottman, New York: Routledge, 2000.

3 INDEFINITE DETENTION

1. "Detention, Treatment, and Trial of Certain Non-Citizens in the War Against Terrorism," Department of Defense, December 12, 2001. This statement clarifies the statement made on November

13 by President Bush announcing the creation of military tribunals for non-US citizens (or non-citizens) suspected of engaging in military terrorism.

2. "Governmentality," in *The Foucault Effect: Studies in Governmentality*, ed. Graham Burchell, Colin Gordon, and Peter Miller, Chicago: University of Chicago Press, 1991, pp. 87–104.

3. Foucault clearly said as much when, for instance, he remarked that "we need to see things not in terms of the replacement of a society of sovereignty by a disciplinary society and the subsequent replacement of a disciplinary society by a society of government; in reality, one has a triangle, sovereignty–discipline–government, which has as its primary target the population and as its essential mechanism the apparatuses of security." "Governmentality," p. 102.

4. Walter Benjamin, "Theses on the Philosophy of History," in *Illuminations: Essays and Reflections*, ed. Hannah Arendt, New York: Schocken, 1968, p. 263.

5. Geoffrey Miller made these remarks in a May 24, 2003 interview with David Dennie of the *Daily Telegraph* in Australia. See news.com.au reports from May 26, 2003.

6. "The Governmentality of Tolerance," in Wendy Brown, *Regulating Aversion: A Critique of Tolerance in the Age of Identity*, Princeton: Princeton University Press, forthcoming.

7. Giorgio Agamben, *Homo Sacer: Sovereign Power and Bare Life*, trans. Daniel Heller-Roazen, Stanford: Stanford University Press, 1998.

8. For a discussion of the "state of exception" as a paradigm for government see Giorgio Agamben, *État d'exception: Homo Sacer, II, 1*, Paris: Éditions du Seuil, 2003, pp. 1–55. See also the section entitled "Life that Does Not Deserve to Live" in *Homo Sacer: Sovereign Power and Bare Life*, pp. 136–43.

9. Department of Defense, March 21, 2002.

10. If the prisoners are being detained to protect them (and others) for their faulty mental functioning, then it is surely paradoxical that the mental health of prisoners deteriorated excessively during the first year and half of their incarceration. Two dozen prisoners reportedly attempted suicide through hanging or strangling themselves, and several engaged in hunger strikes. Apparently one man who attempted to kill himself remains in a coma at the time of this writing. And another is alleged by the *Guardian*, July 20, 2003, to have died in the course of an interrogation session whose tactics appear to conform to the definition of torture.

11. "Some Detainees Held on Guantanamo Are Young Foot Soldiers Caught Up in the Afghan War, US Officials Say," Associated Press, March 29, 2002.

12. For an excellent consideration of the criteria for determining human consideration and its applicability to the Guantanamo prisons, see *Human Rights Watch Backgrounder*, January 29, 2002.

13. The American Bar Association expressed its unwillingness (July, 2003) to encourage lawyers to take on the defense of six detainees marked for trials because they did not want their participation to be construed as an agreement that these tribunals are legitimate.

4   THE CHARGE OF ANTI-SEMITISM: JEWS, ISRAEL, AND THE RISKS OF PUBLIC CRITIQUE

1. David Gelles, "Summers Says Anti-Semitism Lurks Locally," *Harvard Crimson*, September 19, 2002. The full transcript can be found at www.yucommentator.com/v67i4/israelcorner/address.html.

2. Remarks reported in the *Boston Globe*, October 16, 2002.

3. For an extended discussion of how Zionism itself has come to rely upon and perpetuate the notion that Jews, and only Jews, can be

victims, see Adi Ophir, "The Identity of the Victims and the Victims of Identity: A Critique of Zionist Ideology for a Post-Zionist Age," in Laurence Silberstein, ed., *Mapping Jewish Identities*, New York: New York University Press, 2000.

4. Robert Fisk writes, "The all-purpose slander of 'anti-semitism' is now being used with ever-increasing promiscuity against people who condemn the wickedness of Palestinian suicide bombings every bit as much as they do the cruelty of Israel's repeated killing of children in an effort to shut [those people] up." "How to Shut Up Your Critics With a Single Word," *The Independent*, October 21, 2002.

5. Note in the full version of the statement offered as an epigraph to this essay how Summers couples anti-Semitism and anti-Israeli views: "Where anti-Semitism and views that are profoundly anti-Israel have traditionally been the primary reserve of poorly educated right-wing populists, profoundly anti-Israeli views are increasingly finding support in progressive intellectual communities." In this statement he begins by coupling anti-Semitism with anti-Israeli views, without precisely saying that they are the same. But by the end of the sentence, anti-Semitism is absorbed into and carried by the term "anti-Israeli" (rather then anti-*Israel*, as if it were the people who are opposed, rather than the state apparatus) so that we are given to understand not only that anti-Israeli positions, but anti-Semitism itself is finding support among progressive intellectual communities.

6. One can see this letter and its signatories at www.peacemideast.org.

7. See Adi Ophir's discussion of Uri Ram's vision of post-Zionism: "For the post-Zionist, nationality should not determine citizenship, but vice-versa: citizenship should determine the boundaries of the Israeli nation. Judaism would then be regarded as a religion, a community affair, or a matter of a particular ethnicity, one among many." Adi Ophir, "The Identity of the Victims and the Victims of

Identity," p. 186. See also Uri Ram's contribution along with other pieces in Laurence Silberstein, *The Postzionist Debates: Knowledge and Power in Israeli Culture*, New York: Routledge, 1999.

8. AIPAC , the America Israel Public Affairs Committee, is the largest Jewish lobby in the US and is almost always supportive of Israel in its current form and practices.

9. See www.brittzedek.org.

10. See www.ffipp.org.

11. See http://oasisofpeace.org.

12. See www.ipcri.org.

13. See www.btselem.org and www.gush-shalom.org.

14. See www.shministim.org for information on Yesh Gvel. See also Ronit Chacham, *Breaking Ranks: Refusing to Serve in the West Bank and Gaza*, New York: The Other Press, 2003.

15. See http://taayush.tripod.com. Citation quoted with the permission of the author.

16. Yitzhak Iaor, "Will the Circle Be Unbroken?" *Ha'aretz*, August 2, 2002.

5 PRECARIOUS LIFE

1. Emmanuel Levinas and Richard Kearney, "Dialogue with Emmanuel Levinas," in *Face to Face with Levinas*, Albany: SUNY Press, 1986, pp. 23–4. Levinas develops this conception first in *Totality and Infinity: An Essay on Exteriority*, trans. Alphonso Lingis, Pittsburgh: Duquesne University Press, 1969, pp. 187–203. I cull quotations from his later work because I believe they give a more mature and incisive formulation of the face.

2. Emmanuel Levinas, *Ethics and Infinity*, trans. Richard A. Cohen, Pittsburgh: Duquesne University Press, 1985, p. 87. Cited in the text

as *EI*.

3. Emmanuel Levinas, "Peace and Proximity," in *Basic Philosophical Writings*, ed. Adriaan T. Peperzak, Simon Critchley, and Robert Bernasconi, Bloomington: Indiana University Press, 1996. p. 167. Cited in the text as PP.

4. The theological background of this can be found in Exodus. God makes clear to Moses that no one can see God's face, that is, that the divine face is not for seeing and not available to representation: "Thou canst not see my face: for there shall no man see me, and live" (33: 20, *King James*); later, God makes plain that the back can and will substitute for the face: "And I will take away mine hand, and thou shalt see my back parts; but my face shall not be seen" (33: 23). Later, when Moses is carrying God's words in the form of the commandments, it is written, "And when Aaron and all the children of Israel saw Moses, behold, the skin of his face shone; and they were afraid to come nigh him" (34: 30). But Moses' face, carrying the divine word, is also not to be represented. When Moses returns to his human place, he can show his face: "And till Moses had done speaking with them, he put a veil on his face. But when Moses went in before the Lord to speak with him, he came out, and spake unto the children of Israel that which he was commanded. And the children of Israel saw the face of Moses, that the skin of Moses' face shone: and Moses put the veil on his face again, until he went in to speak with him." I thank Barbara Johnson for calling these passages to my attention.

5. Levinas writes, "But that face facing me, in its expression—in its mortality—summons me, demands me, requires me: as if the invisible death faced by the face of the other ... were 'my business.' As if, unknown by the other whom already, in the nakedness of his face, it concerns, it 'regarded me' before its confrontation with me, before being the death that stares me, myself, in the face. The death

of the other man puts me on the spot, calls me into question, as if I, by my possible indifference, became the accomplice of that death, invisible to the other who is exposed to it; as if even before being condemned to it myself, I had to answer for that death of the other, and not leave the other alone to his deathly solitude," in Emmanuel Levinas, *Alterity and Transcendence*, New York: Columbia University Press, 1999, pp. 24–5.

6. Levinas distinguishes sometimes between the "countenance" understood as the face within perceptual experience, and the "face" whose coordinates are understood to transcend the perceptual field. He also speaks on occasion about "plastic" representations of the face that efface the face. For the face to operate as a face, it must vocalize or be understood as the workings of a voice.

7. See Lila Abu-Lughod, "Do Muslim Women Really Need Saving? Anthropological Reflections on Cultural Relativism and Others," *American Anthropologist*, 104: 3, pp. 783–90.

8. For an extended discussion of the relation between the media image and human suffering, see Susan Sontag's provocative *Regarding the Pain of Others*, New York: Farrar, Straus, and Giroux, 2002.

9. For a discussion of "failure" as basic to a psychoanalytic conception of the psyche, see Jacqueline Rose, *Sexuality in the Field of Vision*, London: Verso, 1986, pp. 91–3.

10. Levinas writes, "one can say that the face is not 'seen.' It is what cannot become a content, which your thought would embrace; it is uncontainable, it leads you beyond" (*EI*, pp. 86–7).

INDEX